THE MEANINGS
OF LOVE

THE MEANINGS
OF LOVE

&

*An Introduction to Philosophy
of Love*

ROBERT E. WAGONER

For Paul & Louise —

Bob Wagoner

PRAEGER

Westport, Connecticut
London

Library of Congress Cataloging-in-Publication Data

Wagoner, Bob, 1930–
    The meanings of love : an introduction to philosophy of love /
    Robert E. Wagoner.
        p.   cm.
    Includes bibliographical references and index.
        ISBN 0–275–95839–6 (alk. paper). — ISBN 0–275–95840–X (pbk. :
    alk. paper)
        1. Love.   2. Love—History.   I. Title.
    BD436.W34   1997
    128'.46—dc21   96–37115

British Library Cataloguing in Publication Data is available.

Library of Congress Catalog Card Number: 96–37115
ISBN: 0–275–95839–6
      0–275–95840–X (pbk.)

First published in 1997

Praeger Publishers, 88 Post Road West, Westport, CT 06881
An imprint of Greenwood Publishing Group, Inc.

Printed in the United States of America

The paper used in this book complies with the
Permanent Paper Standard issued by the National
Information Standards Organization (Z39.48–1984).

10 9 8 7 6 5 4 3 2 1

Copyright Acknowledgments

The author and publisher gratefully acknowledge permission for use of the following material:

"The Mess of Love" by D. H. Lawrence, edited by V. de Sola Pinto & F. W. Roberts, from THE COMPLETE POEMS OF D. H. LAWRENCE by D. H. Lawrence, edited by V. de Sola Pinto & F. W. Roberts. Copyright © 1964, 1971 by Angelo Ravagli and C. M. Weekley, Executors of the Estate of Frieda Lawrence Ravagli. Used by permission of Viking Penguin, a division of Penguin Books USA, Inc.

Translation of Gottfried of Strasbourg's *Tristan* by Denis de Rougemont, *Love in the Western World* (Pantheon Books, 1956), page 146, note 1. Copyright © 1956 by Pantheon Books. Used by permission of Random House, Inc.

"September 1, 1939," from W. H. AUDEN: COLLECTED POEMS by W. H. Auden, edited by Edward Mendelson. Copyright © 1940 by W. H. Auden. Reprinted by permission of Random House, Inc.

CONTENTS

PREFACE

The good news about love is that it makes life meaningful. The bad news is that there is always a price to be paid. "Free love" is an oxymoron—a contradiction in terms. Moreover, this seems to be true regardless of the diverse meanings that love has for us.

There is legitimate disagreement about what love means. One cannot fairly assume that this is due merely to ignorance or perversity. This book assumes that love has more than one meaning and that the first task is to sort out what these meanings are. The second task is to see what each meaning requires.

Why a person is captive to one idea rather than another I do not attempt to explain, nor do I argue that one idea is necessarily better than another. Each of the six ideas of love sketched out here is problematic—that is, each is ideal in its own way, but each is limiting in a certain way as well. Where there is no limit, there is no meaning.

The discussion of each idea focuses on how love is defined, therefore, and shows what this meaning implies for both our physical and our rational natures. Even though each idea of love is considered separately, and can be read alone, there are continuities from one idea to another as a sequence of ideas is developed.

The study of other peoples' ideas of love, even those of great thinkers, is of course only preliminary to thinking about our own experiences. To this end I have striven, perhaps too much, to simplify and clarify these ideas as much as possible. Further inquiry and reflection will reveal pretty quickly that the primary sources are much richer than I have represented them and that real life is never quite so neat.

I have been helped in this approach by the give and take of countless classroom discussions. There is no better arena for testing the clarity, consistency, and viability of ideas so close to the heart. But even more, some early drafts of these studies benefited from careful reviews given to me by student tutors Mary Fortson and Janine Hyde. Later drafts were improved by the many thoughtful and sensitive suggestions I received from colleagues, especially Grace Fala and Donna Weimer. Most of all I am indebted to Judy Katz, colleague in the English Department, whose many helps I could not have done without. Her constant support, gentle prodding, and patient questioning kept the book alive when it was in danger of being stillborn. Thanks also to Bill Russey and Jarmila Polte for frequent computer rescue missions, and especially to Art Manion, whose technical skills were indispensable in getting the manuscript to its final form. The index was prepared by my wife, Shirley Wagoner, to whom I am grateful for yet another instance of the deictic role she has played in my life. For help in getting this project launched I owe thanks to former academic dean Karen Sandler, and to Graydon F. Snyder, formerly of the Chicago Theological Seminary, and especially to Robert W. Neff, president of Juniata College, for his unqualified endorsement and unflagging insistence that I see the book into publication.

Robert E. Wagoner
Juniata College
Huntingdon, Pennsylvania

Chapter 1

&

INTRODUCTION

We've made a great mess of love
Since we made an ideal of it.

— D. H. Lawrence

What a muddle love is.

Love is everywhere celebrated as the most important experience in human life. Who would argue against love? Whether it brings great joy or great suffering, there are few who would deny that the presence of love can fill life with meaning and purpose, and the absence of love can turn life into an empty desert.

Almost as widespread, however, are the complaints about love's confusions and contradictions. How can such a great human good have so many unintended consequences and be so hard to understand? If "Love is all you need," as the Beatles used to sing, why does it seem to go wrong so often? Why does something that seems so clear involve so many contradictions? How can something that means so much to me be so much out of my control? Try as we might, we do not seem to understand love very well.

My intent in writing this book is not to try to plumb the psychological mysteries of love. That would be quite beyond me. But I believe at least part of our confusion about love is due to the way we think about it—and my intent here is to try to clarify some of our most important ideas about love.

At the bottom of the confusion, I think, is the basic fact that love is a relationship—a relationship between ourselves and others. A loving relationship is unlike other relationships, however, not only in the degree of its importance but also because it is fundamentally paradoxical. The more important the relationship is, the more important the other is to me. The paradox is that love simultaneously involves interest in oneself with interest in another. The similarities and the differences of the two interests are what engage one's attention—but the point is that they are two different interests.

Moreover, I find that caring about another has the curious effect of making me more aware of myself. But my increased self-awareness is linked to an interest outside myself in another person. To love is not only to have divided interests, but also to be out of control of those interests. No wonder love is confusing if it is essentially the relation of who I am with who somebody else is.

Perhaps this paradox is not as extreme in some cultures as it is in our own. In some societies the primary emphasis is not on a highly individuated self, but on family or clan or caste. Self-interest and the other's interest are not clearly differentiated because the collective values of the society are uppermost. The meaning of my life is not something that I must find for myself; to a large extent it is already given because of my membership in the larger group. Nor are the intimate relations with other people something that I must work out for myself for they are likely to be governed by family, caste, and class considerations. The question of love either does not come up at all or takes a back seat to priorities already established.

The prominence of love in Western culture, by contrast, may be directly correlated to the high value we give to the development of unique personality. The greater the emphasis on individuality, the greater the degree of differentiation, of separateness. Indeed, one might say that the more highly individualized a person is, the more alienated he or she is. This is the problem that love seeks to solve: how shall the self, virtually isolated in the individuality so highly prized, form a relation with other isolated selves?

For us, therefore, the fundamental problem that love seeks to solve is loneliness—the separateness of the self. Whoever said that "love is finding oneself in another" has provided a fairly good definition of the general meaning of love in Western culture and makes fairly obvious the extent to which love and selfhood are inextricably linked together. The paradox of love turns out to have two dimensions: the solution to the problem of loneliness creates the problem of divided interests, and this, in turn, poses the problem of identity. Am I a self if I do not find myself in another — that is, am I lost or incomplete? And am I still myself if I do find myself in another — that is, have I given up my individuality?

The main reason, therefore, that love is so terribly important in Western culture is that the very nature of the self is at issue and our most important ideas about love seem to revolve around this problem. My intention in this book is to survey the main ideas about love that have emerged from the paradox of finding one's self in another: erotic love, Christian love, romantic love, moral love, love as power, and mutual love. My approach is not historical as such, although I do not ignore some of the obvious ways in which history has furthered the development of some ideas. My focus is on the structure of these ideas, on what makes them internally coherent, and on what is distinctive about each one.

In order to compile this inventory of major ideas of love in the Western tradition, I rely on some of the most prominent writers and philosophers, both ancient and modern, who have helped to shape and articulate them. While the authors selected may not necessarily have been the first or the only ones to express these ideas, they are without exception extraordinarily original, eloquent, and powerful in the ways they define and resolve love's dilemma of one self finding itself in another. Each chapter, therefore, leans heavily on these primary sources in an attempt to make their inner consistency as explicit as possible. At best, however, these are only brief, introductory presentations and by no means exhaust the richness of what these authors have to say.

These concepts deserve critical examination, I believe, because they make up the repertoire of ideas available to us when we think about love. When we try to make sense of our experience of love, one of these ideas, or some combination of them, comes into play and governs our thinking. There may or may not be much logic to our experience, but there is a logic to ideas and this is what I focus on.

THE SIX IDEAS

One of the oldest ideas of love in the Western tradition and also the first to define love flatly and unequivocally in terms of enlightened self-interest is Plato's concept of erotic love. Plato's intent is to show how erotic love is not simply identical with sexual desire, but drives far beyond it in the quest for perfection. His view is sometimes referred to as "classical," not only because historians designate his time period with this term, but also because Plato's characterization of love as the striving for what is best and most beautiful has set a high standard against which other ideas are measured. Plato's views have not gone unchallenged, of course, but no one can think seriously about love without dealing with his insights. The identification of self-interest with excellence has become authoritative for us.

The second idea is diametrically opposite to love as self-interest: it is the Christian concept of love as utter selflessness. This concept of love is more difficult to understand than Plato's because one must first grasp how the love of others depends upon the prior relationship to that which is "wholly other" — God. Both Plato and Christian writers agree that love is essential to human nature, but they radically disagree about what this means. According to Plato, we love what we do not have — beauty, truth, and goodness — and the meaning of life is determined by how intelligently we pursue these desires. According to Christians, we love what we do have — God-given freedom — and the meaning of life is determined by the gift of that freedom to others. Through the centuries many people have found the idea of Christian love more compelling than Plato's because it suggests that human personality is best understood not in terms of what it gets but in terms of what it gives. The utmost expression of love is the utmost gift of the self. There is something awe inspiring about this, even though it appears almost self-contradictory to imply that selflessness is the epitome of what it means to be human.

Not only is Christian love difficult to comprehend, but it comes to us refracted through many different sources, many of which are touched by Plato's influence. Christianity emerged in classical times, after all, and the New Testament was originally written in Greek. Moreover, the texts we rely on, from the Bible and the early church fathers, are additionally ambiguous because what is said about love is complicated by many other problems of concern to the early Christian communities. One could argue quite legitimately that the mystery of Christian love exceeds any attempt at definition. While I do not disagree with this, I think there is an underlying thread of affirmation, which begins with "the image of God" in the book of Genesis and continues through the Gospels and the letters of the apostle Paul, that helps us to see why Christians say the other in which we find ourselves can only be the "divine other."

When we say, therefore, that "love is finding oneself in another," Plato and Christianity are the two main sources for the meanings that fall out of this paradoxical definition. Virtually all of our main ideas about love are shaped by the way in which the two contrary impulses of self-interest and self-giving are brought together. To find oneself in another necessarily involves both these considerations, sometimes leaning more heavily on one, sometimes on the other. Neither of these concepts entirely resolves the dilemma, but each shows us something quite distinctive about what love means.

The third idea, romantic love, is easily the best known idea of love in the popular imagination. This is odd, in a way, because its origins were aristocratic, having to do with the lords and ladies of the Middle Ages, but through songs and poetry its appeal soon spread to all social classes and still dominates the way we think about love. Why? The secret of the power of romantic love is that it makes love a religion. This is where its magic comes from. It is a remarkable synthesis of erotic love and Christian love. When I examine the story of Tristan and Iseult and the letters of Heloise and Abelard, I look for the way absolute devotion (self-giving) is combined with erotic longing (self-interest) so that their lives are unforgettably transformed. Romantic lovers do indeed find themselves in each other—but usually with devastating results.

The otherworldliness of romantic love, with its ecstatic disregard of consequences, leads necessarily to a consideration of its opposite, to a view of love whose inner principle is stability and moral uprightness. This is the fourth idea of love I consider—"true love" or moral love. One could argue that any idea of love is "true" (i.e., consistent) within the perspective of that idea, but the phrase "true love" is generally distinguished from other meanings by its special emphasis on faithfulness and integrity. Two strong spokesmen for this view of love are Immanuel Kant and Søren Kierkegaard. Both take seriously the dilemma posed by an independent and self-governing self finding itself in another. How can an autonomous consciousness overcome its isolation and make a true and faithful relation to another? Can it then still be autonomous? The solutions forged by Kant and Kierkegaard differ somewhat, but are similar in the way they shape a model of human character that commands our respect. What they show us, however, is that when the idea of true love is examined rigorously the demands it lays upon us may be both more extreme and less satisfying than we bargained for.

The fifth idea of love, love as power, also turns on the dilemma of the isolated self but is much more ambiguous because it takes account of the shifting dynamics involved in finding myself in another. To put it simply, the other has power over me because I need him or her. Without the recognition of the other I have no sense of my self, but this means that I endlessly vacillate between desire and fear—desire for the other's acknowledgment, and fear that it may be withdrawn. What we call love is thus unmasked as a desperate power struggle—not unlike Thomas Hobbes's "war of every man against every man"—because one's very being is at stake. This is a dark picture of love, to be sure, but there is no doubt that Jean-Paul Sartre's extensive analysis of the conflicted nature of love goes far to illumine the perpetual insecurity that seems to be so characteristic of most loving relationships. Sartre shows us what happens when the freedom of the self has no way to understand itself except by way of another's freedom.

The sixth, and final, idea implied by the paradox of finding oneself in another is an idea of equilibrium between the self and the other: mutual love. This idea originated with Aristotle, who was a student of Plato's and later a philosophical rival, but we shall consider it at this point as a possible response to the unhappy power struggle that Sartre leaves with us. The question is whether, in the face of maneuvers of fear and desire, genuine mutuality can be achieved. In order to broaden the relevance of this discussion, as well as to gain a different critical perspective, I shall also include the thinking of Luce Irigaray, a contemporary French psychiatrist and philosopher, who is well known for her original work on the problem of sexual identity and her critical reappraisal of both classical and modern authorities on this issue. Despite the sharp differences between Aristotle and Irigaray, a concept of mutual love emerges from this somewhat unlikely comparison.

THE STRUCTURE OF THESE IDEAS

In order to see what the crucial issues are in each idea, and to see them comparatively, the principal focus of each chapter is, first, on how one's relationship with the other is defined, and, second, on how this external relation involves our mental life and physical life—specifically our rational natures and our sexual natures. If an idea of love hangs together there should be a consistent connection between the defining form of the relationship and these two dimensions of human experience. To make this coherent structure as explicit as possible each of the subsequent six chapters follows the same format.

Since the problem that love seeks to solve is the isolation of the self, the key consideration in each case is the nature of the relationship by which one finds himself or herself in another. In each chapter, therefore, following an introductory discussion, the first section is "The Defining Relation." In most loving relationships this is rarely made explicit, at least initially, because it is usually sufficient simply to recognize that one loves the other. Yet these unspoken assumptions establish an underlying logic that sooner or later determines everything else about the relationship. To have a meaningful relationship with someone is to acknowledge that certain definitions and priorities have been established that give it an ongoing consistency.

How is the connection made between myself and the other? The real answer to this question is probably inaccessible—buried too deeply in our emotions and psychological destinies ever to comprehend very clearly. But how do we think the connection is made? That is, is love rational, or at least compatible with reason, or is it fundamentally contrary to reason, maybe even superior to reason? The second section of each chapter, "The Role of Reason," focuses on this issue. If there is some rational basis for why I find myself in another, then presumably such a relationship could be explained and defended as well as criticized and judged. If love is fundamentally irrational or nonrational, then it is its own justification. These are difficult questions, and the answers are not always clear, but addressing them does throw additional light on the distinguishing character of each idea of love.

The corollary to the question of love and reason is the whimsical question that the humorist, James Thurber, used to put: "Is sex necessary?" Despite its biological importance, sex seems to be invariably problematic with regard to love. The next section of each chapter, "The Role of Sexuality," deals with the troublesome relation between love and sexual desire, and also such issues as gender roles and heterosexuality and homosexuality.

The initial focus of each chapter is on interpersonal love because for most people, most of the time, this is what it means to find oneself in another. But the fourth section of each chapter, "Outcomes," extends the logic of the core structure of each idea a bit further to show what follows from it. In some cases the larger and more abstract meanings of love, such as love of country or love of mankind or, even, love of God do not seem to be implied, whereas in the cases of Plato, Aristotle, and Christianity they seem to be necessary outcomes.

The fifth and final section of each chapter, "Assessment," does not evaluate these ideas of love in terms of which is better or which is worse—morally, psychologically, or whatever—but briefly summarizes the kind of meaning to be expected from each idea. It is important to see that the logic that produces one meaning usually precludes others.

THE INTEGRITY OF THESE IDEAS

In examining these six ideas of love, therefore, I assume that each has its own legitimacy. After all, when one is in love, it seems good to him or to her. No one who is actually in love ever thinks that his or her love is childish, or false, or ignoble. Others may make such disparaging judgments, or one may later come to be critical of earlier attitudes, but from inside the conviction, each idea is absolutely right.

There is something authoritative about love, although why one embraces one idea rather than another may be very hard to account for. If one has indeed found oneself in another, then that is a very compelling experience and puts an end to dispute. The question is, how has this happened? By establishing what priorities and what logical relationships? This is what this book is about. By coming to understand the underlying structure of the idea of love, one is more likely to see where it is leading, and at what cost and for what benefits. The appeal of each idea is the meaning it provides, but each also imposes certain constraints that may be hard to bear. Love is no free lunch.

I should point out that these are discussions of ideas of love, not about any of the institutional forms that love might take. That is, this discussion is not about marriage or family life or dating practices as such. Despite the popular song that says that "love and marriage go together like a horse and carriage" we know that this is not so. Marriages can endure quite well without being love matches, and it seems equally obvious that love affairs can flourish without fitting any regularized social pattern. My focus is on what love means to us—on its logical forms, as it were, and not on its social forms. I shall not try to resolve the question of whether social structures generate ideas or whether ideas produce social structures.

At the highest level of generality, perhaps the six different meanings of love sketched out in this book could be reconciled so that they are all shown to be aspects of the same thing—although I have to wonder how much meaning such an abstraction would have. At the opposite extreme, it is not too difficult to demonstrate that every use of the word "love" is unique—no two people could mean exactly the same thing by it. In the absence of any common rule of definition or empirical reference, the very plurality of possible meanings makes the word meaningless.

This book is about an intermediate realm between these two extremes—where discrete meanings can be identified and where these different meanings affect the way we think about love and how we experience love. The intermediate is after all the realm of the common. Love is what we have in common, yet we have to come to terms with the differences in our understanding and learn to live with them.

Chapter 2

℘

EROTIC LOVE: PLATO, *SYMPOSIUM* AND *PHAEDRUS*

Love lures life on.

— Thomas Hardy

The genius of Plato's idea of love is that it begins with our conventional notion of sexual love but then extends our understanding so that we see how this erotic power leads to personal growth and intellectual development, even to the passion for science and political order. Erotic love, he shows us, is not simply sexual desire, but desire understood in a far more fundamental and far-reaching sense. Plato argues this way because he believes, in some very profound sense, that the proper understanding of love is the key to most of our important problems.

Plato lived in ancient Greece in the fourth and fifth centuries before the Christian era, a time as confusing as our own. Public life was in constant turmoil and controversy, war or the threat of war between Greek city-states seemed unending, and new thinking about science and morality appeared to undermine traditional values.

This very diversity of opinions and ideas constituted a problem for Plato. In the midst of so many conflicting claims about what is right or good, how is one to know which to follow? Plato would not concede that it was merely a matter of majority opinion since he had seen his friend and teacher, Socrates, condemned to death by a "democratic" jury simply because Socrates had raised questions that the majority did not like. Obviously, the opinions of the many were not necessarily just or right.

And how was one to resolve the debates among early scientific thinkers about the reality of the material world? Since all material things are subject to change and decay, how "real" are they? Is there some human reality (a soul) that is different from the material world and not subject to change and decay? How should one live one's life in the face of so many uncertainties and confusions? For Plato the answers to these questions were more than a matter for idle speculation. How one thought about these questions determined how one lived.

The opinions of the day were dominated by a group of professional teachers known as sophists—"wise ones." They were quite influential (among those who could afford to pay their fees) because they taught the argumentative skills that were necessary for success in the disputatious public life of democratic Athens. The sophists offered an easy solution to the questions that troubled Plato. Brushing all other considerations aside, they asserted that it was simply a matter of looking out for yourself. If, as Protagoras maintained, "man is the measure of all things," then one should act according to whatever is the most advantageous politically, materially, or whatever. Since all value is relative to the individual, one should pursue one's own self-interest as vigorously as possible. One would be a fool to do otherwise.

Plato saw all too clearly the appeal of such a simplistic approach, but he also saw how it could lead to political chaos as well as personal confusion. Determining just what is in one's interest is not as obvious as might first appear. What is virtue? What is knowledge? What is love? Does the soul survive the death of the body? In the course of a long career Plato wrestled with these and other questions by putting them in the form of dialogues in which his former teacher, Socrates, is presented as the key figure who interrogates well-known persons, some of whom were sophists. Sometimes these dialogues end inconclusively. Conventional beliefs fall apart when they are examined closely, and the participants, including Socrates, are sometimes forced to admit that they do not really know what they thought they knew. On other occasions it is fairly apparent that Plato makes Socrates his spokesman and the dialogue is actually an exposition of certain ideas, not an argument or interrogation.

In either case it is important to note that Plato never gives up the fundamental assumption that finding the truth is a matter of self-interest: I desire the good for myself. Plato does not dispute the sophist teachers on this. What he argues, however, is the true understanding of self-interest. How can I know that what appears to be good is really good? Is there a difference between what is of immediate advantage to me and what is advantageous in the long run?

Plato's dialogues often do not "answer" these questions very satisfactorily because they turn up uncertain definitions and unexpected implications. The dialogues reveal very quickly that our ordinary notions about what matters most to us are shot through with confusion and contradiction. Underlying all the dialogues, however, is Plato's belief that there is a logic to human desires, even if we cannot always find it. Every dialogue proceeds on the assumption that progress can be made by moving beyond what is immediately apparent toward something more comprehensive and more enduring.

A dialogue is not just conversation, it is a *searching* conversation: we have some idea of what we are looking for and some idea of how to look for it. We all have some idea of what is good for us and some idea of what is better and worse. There is, in other words, a logic to what we love, and, if we follow it, we are compelled to see that consistency and coherence are an advance over what is merely particular or momentary. To search for the good carries us beyond immediate satisfaction to what is more lasting, beyond fragmentation to wholeness. When we are putting together a puzzle, even a vague idea of the whole picture is enormously helpful in making sense of the separate pieces. Even if we do not entirely grasp the whole, we know that it takes precedence over the parts. Rational inquiry, therefore, if carried through rigorously, leads us from a narrow perspective of self-interest toward one that is more universal and ideal.

The desire for what is *best* for ourselves reveals that the limited and impermanent experiences of ordinary life have to be measured against a standard of quality in order to know their true worth. The *best* is not necessarily the same as the *easiest* or the *most*. While the ideal is the true object of our search, even in Plato's dialogues it does not always come into view. As in our own lives, what is excellent — truly the best and most beautiful — is sometimes obscured by what is merely conventional or convenient.

In the *Symposium* Plato shows us that this search for the ideal, for beauty itself, is what love is all about. Love is what leads from appearances to reality, love is what connects the immediate to the ultimate. Sometimes Plato subordinates this theme to larger questions of rational and political order, as in the *Republic*; sometimes he disparages the immediate and material in favor of the spiritual, as in the *Phaedo*; but throughout his major works he does not deviate from the conviction that there is a fundamental inclination within every human being to seek, and to love, that which is good for him or her. This is our essential self-interest.

In an early dialogue, *Lysis*, Plato's first attempt at defining love begins and ends by acknowledging its presence, but a consistent grasp of its meaning eludes Socrates and his young friends. It is in the *Phaedrus* and especially in the *Symposium*, his literary and philosophical masterpiece, that Plato succeeds most eloquently in defining love as "eros," the powerful desire for what we lack.

THE DEFINING RELATION

However love is defined, it must be understood as a relation of some kind. Plato sees this relation as essentially erotic, but he shows us that erotic desire and sexual desire are not exactly the same thing. Desire may be initiated by sexual interest but usually there is something more involved. Why this particular person when almost anyone could satisfy a merely sexual appetite? That is, one person loves another because the other signifies something he or she wants. We do not desire what we already have, so love is precisely this desire for what we do not have. Everyone is in pursuit of something or someone he or she does not have. Love is thus the motor of human experience. If we are content with what we are, with what we have, we do not act. It is precisely because we are never quite satisfied, never quite content with the way things are, that we seek something other. Erotic love is restless, it energizes us, it keeps us on the move. Without love we would come to a dead stop.

Plato's basic assumption about human nature is that we are "needy" beings. There is something insufficient, incomplete, about human nature. We relate to one another, to anything and to everything, because we are in want. Everyone in this sense is a lover.

This is exactly why love is so confusing. We have many different kinds of desires. We love ice cream, we love our family and friends, we love honor and integrity. Are not these very different kinds of love? In fact, isn't there a direct conflict between the love of pleasure and material things and the love of moral and spiritual things?

In the *Symposium* Plato takes up these questions by describing a drinking party attended by prominent Athenians, including Socrates. The subject for the evening's entertainment is "love" and each man presents a little speech giving his views. The mood is lighthearted. It is a party, after all, and they speak informally, even though there are rivalries among those present and each man is competing to give the best speech. As is often the case in Plato's dialogues, the speeches begin with rather conventional platitudes, but with each successive speaker something of an intellectual ascent begins to take place. The differences and contradictions that emerge push our understanding of love along as the speeches progress.

The first speaker is Phaedrus, after whom Plato names his other major dialogue on love. Speaking in praise of love, Phaedrus strings together mostly trite and self-serving sentiments, without much regard for consistency. Love is an ancient god, he says, who bestows great gifts, the greatest being that of a gentle lover for a boy.[1] It is not hard to tell what Phaedrus has in mind. Even so, Phaedrus sets the tone for what is to follow by declaring love to be a divine power that improves men by making them desire to appear good and noble to their beloved, even to the point of death.

Pausanias, who follows, faces head-on the problem of conflicting desires. Love is divine, he agrees, but it is duality, not a single power. He declares that "there are two Aphrodites" (two goddesses of love) who require a distinction between "common love," which is of the body, and "heavenly love," which is the love of wisdom and excellence. Like Phaedrus, his intent is to justify the love of a young boy by an older man by cleverly idealizing its benefits as "heavenly" and disdaining mere lust and wantonness as "common." While Pausanias's sophistic argument is not very convincing, it nonetheless confronts the common dilemma of conflicting loves and points the way to a solution by elevating one meaning above the other.

The next speaker, Eryximachus, who is a physician, tries to overcome this problem with a naturalistic account of love as a cosmic principle—a harmony of discordant elements in human experience. Both kinds of love are therefore necessary, he says, but in proper combination and proportion.

The following speaker is Aristophanes, the well-known comic playwright, who handles the double nature of love in an entirely different way. The picture he presents is amusing but nonetheless insightful. For Aristophanes, love is not a divine power but rather the reunion of what is separated. To convey this notion he tells the story of how human beings were originally round, with four arms, four feet, and a head with two faces. Because of their strength and arrogance, Zeus punished them by cutting them in two. Ever since, the two halves have longed for each other, and this desire to be reunited is love.

Despite the ridiculous picture that this calls up before us, many people intuitively agree with Aristophanes' point. When love draws us to another, it is because we see ourselves in the other person. He or she is essential to our identity. We are not complete without the other person. We love him or her not because they are "other," someone different from us, but because they are innately our own. In the strictest sense, says Aristophanes, the other person is "meant for us" (193b).

I suspect that the reason Plato presents this view so comically is that the idea is very close to his own view, and by putting it in the mouth of Aristophanes it is dialectically differentiated from what Socrates later says. When Aristophanes declares that "love is the name for our pursuit of wholeness, for our desire to be complete" (193a), it is only a small step to the Socratic view that love seeks the good. But it is important to see that wholeness in itself is not necessarily desirable unless it also happens to be good. Wholeness might not be in our self-interest, for example, if that includes a diseased limb. The good, in this case, might mean amputation. Thus, Socrates agrees with Aristophanes' statement that love leads us "towards what belongs to us" (193d) but moves the argument one step higher to show that "what belongs to us" is the good, not necessarily the whole (205e).

The good that all men seek is necessarily beautiful, says Agathon, the speaker who immediately precedes Socrates, because love never seeks what is ugly. Agathon's eloquent tribute to love as the youngest and most beautiful of the gods makes love and beauty interchangeable. Once again, this sets the stage for Socrates to move the argument forward by distinguishing between the nature of love (what it is) and its object (what it seeks). In the *Phaedrus* love is first awakened by the power of beauty because of its vivid appeal to the clearest of our senses — sight. Wisdom, however, does not present such a clear image of itself in the world.[2]

What then is the good that we seek? What is the object of our desire? What we lack most fundamentally is *being*. That is, human nature in and of itself lacks substance. To be human is to be mortal, limited, subject to change. We are born and we die. We can do this or that, we can possess this or that, but we cannot be — simply and wholly and without limit or variation. The object of love is thus perpetual being, immortality. What we want is to be — eternally. This is why love is always pledged "forever." To say that we will love someone for a limited time (say, for six months) or in a limited way (with half a heart) seems self-contradictory. Love is eternal and total or it is not love.

In the *Symposium* Socrates makes the surprising statement fairly early that "the only thing I say I understand is the art of love" (177e). This is puzzling because in other dialogues Socrates always claims to know nothing. His reputation as the wisest man in Athens is due to his ready admission that he knows that he knows nothing. When we realize, however, that love is a lack, a desire for what we do not have, then it makes sense for Socrates to say that love is the only subject he understands. This is what a "philosopher" is — one who loves (seeks) wisdom because he does not have it. His position is somewhere *between* knowledge and ignorance. Neither the wise nor the ignorant desire to know because they are satisfied with where they are. Only the philosopher (Socrates) who understands his ignorance desires to go beyond it.

Therefore Socrates needs a teacher, and he confesses that what he knows about love he learned from Diotima, a woman of Matinea (201d). Plato never really tells us who she is. For Socrates to acknowledge *any* teacher is surprising, and that it should be a woman is even more surprising if we recall the male-dominated, even homoerotic, atmosphere in which the discussion takes place.

There are no women present in the *Symposium*, and, indeed, women are not present generally in the public life of classical Greece. But it is noteworthy that through Socrates a woman's voice is heard and it is through this woman's voice that a very important dialectical transition is made.

So far the mood of the *Symposium* has been one of playful eroticism, but Diotima's voice (through Socrates) gives a more serious turn to the conversation. Not surprisingly, what Diotima "teaches" Socrates, he already knows. His awareness of what he lacks is what makes him listen. One cannot answer questions that have not been asked. It is only when we know that we are in need that we can learn. Diotima's instruction consists of naming and conceptualizing the yearning within Socrates by directing attention to male-to-female sexual reproduction instead of the male-to-male erotic relationships that have been the subject of conversation up to this point. Love is rooted in the urge to procreate, she points out, a desire we share with all animals and so powerful that we would give up our lives to carry it out (207b). But she then redefines the significance of sexual reproduction as the quest for immortality and not mere biological perpetuity (208b).

Through a woman's voice, in other words, the discussion turns to the most elemental level of natural function but is then elevated to transcend altogether the level of physical nature. Diotima shows that the search for the meaning of love cannot be understood within the play of male-to-male eroticism but only from the female perspective, which apprehends that its true significance is to overcome the limit of human fatality. What love truly seeks is to escape death.

Diotima begins by reminding Socrates that the desire for immortality is what draws men to women, to beget children and achieve a kind of physical immortality by perpetuating themselves genetically (206c). At another level, however, this desire is what draws us toward a particularly attractive individual, to possess her or his beauty for ourselves and to realize our selves through it (209bc). Having achieved this, we are then able to appreciate this quality more broadly in other individuals and the individualizing characteristics themselves become irrelevant (210ab). We are then ready to move to a still higher level. Gradually we realize that physical beauty is transcended by moral beauty and intellectual beauty because the latter two are more universal, more enduring, and less susceptible to change and decay. What we ultimately want for ourselves, of course, is beyond time and change (211a) — that which is good and beautiful and true without qualification.

Surprisingly, therefore, erotic love turns out to be ascetic in its basic principle. It is *disciplined* desire, not mere lustful appetite. It may be initiated in sexual desire, but erotic love gradually and inevitably pulls away from the level of physical gratification in its search for qualities more enduring.

In its best light, erotic love is the passionate commitment to all that is good and true and beautiful. This is its essential interest because this is what is most real. That there is a certain "inhuman" quality about it, however, is hard to deny, since it seeks an ideal of perfection, not particular persons or objects as such. Every erotic relationship is thus inevitably transient in nature. Irving Singer puts it cogently: "All beauties attract, but none can really satisfy... Man transcends himself by a *lack of fidelity* to the objects of his present interest, which frustrate merely in being finite and thus incapable of satisfying his infinite appetite."[3]

The essential point in Plato's idea of love is that love is not an end in itself but a means to an end. Love is not itself beautiful, as Agathon had maintained in the *Symposium*; love is the desire *for* the beautiful. Love is personified by Diotima as an intermediary — neither divine nor human but "something between the two." He is "a great spirit," she says, a *daimon* who bridges the gap between the divine and the human, and binds the universe together (202e-203a). It is the lack of the divine, the perfect, the good in ourselves that leads us to seek it in another. It is more than a sense of incompleteness, like searching for a missing piece of a puzzle, because that would be a limited desire, a search for a discrete and particular object, and what Plato is talking about cannot be satisfied by any particular thing or individual.

THE ROLE OF REASON

What happens to the erotic lover is the enlightenment of his desire. Under the power of love we learn first to discriminate among the qualities of physical things, then to seek the qualities themselves, and finally to seek the highest form of these qualities — perfection itself. It is an educational, or developmental, process. The sophisticated lover becomes more and more discriminating as he learns about each new object of desire — what it is and what it is not. Each new relationship pulls him along a little further in his quest. Thus, as long as he loves, he is learning. Love and reason are almost the same thing.

In the *Symposium* this is how Plato overcomes the problem of the double nature of love, first introduced by Pausanias: love of the physical versus love of the spiritual. Love of what is physical and individual does not pull against love of what is spiritual and ideal, but is rather a means, a steppingstone, toward the latter. In the *Phaedrus* we are told that there are two guiding principles within us: an innate desire for pleasure and an acquired judgment that aims at what is best. The first is wanton and irrational and must be constantly restrained by the second (238). Desire becomes rational because it must distinguish between what is merely good and what is best. Reason collects and divides — it shows us similarities and differences, Socrates says later in the *Phaedrus* (265–266). Discriminating love apprehends the new in terms of what we already know and discloses what would be better or worse. Love always seeks what is beyond, what it does not have.

"Thus we are continually shown the reality of what is better and the illusory nature of what is worse," says Iris Murdoch. "We learn of perfection and imperfection through our ability to understand what we see as an image or shadow of something better which we cannot yet see."[4] Erotic love, if we are serious about it, compels us to be critical and moves us forward. The affirmation of new love carries within it a negation of the old love. The new level of desire disdains where it had been before and could not return to it.

This is also how Plato resolves the problem of sophist relativism. That love is a matter of self-interest seems obvious. What love seeks is the good for oneself. No one would argue that we should love what is boring or what is in someone else's interest. But some things are better than others and it is the business of love to discern to what extent a new desire is better than the previous one. Does it elevate our sensibilities? Does it bring new insight? Is it more universal in its grasp? Is it more enduring and less vulnerable to change?

There is a sense, then, in which love is infallible — it always seeks the good.[5] Mistakes are made not because we love what is wrong, but because we are ignorant of the limitations or the

consequences of what we desire. Appearances deceive us. As
lovers we have to learn to distinguish between what appears to be
good and what is really in our self-interest. That is, we learn to be
rational.

Each person must begin where he is—his first love. While the
process described by Diotima is generally the same for everyone,
its actual realization is unique to each person. Exactly why we
have a particular passion may be inexplicable, the subject of endless
psychological speculation. In the *Phaedrus* Plato says, "every one
chooses his love from the ranks of beauty according to his
character" (252d). In the *Lysis*, Plato suggests that the "first
instance" of love or "first love" is actually something original to
our nature, something that "belongs" to us and is the true object
of all our loving relations.[6] The yearning in love, therefore, is for
our own true self. L. A. Kosman says, "Erotic love is thus primarily
for Plato *self-love*, for it is finally our true self which is once native
to us and lacked by us."[7] The point is what we learn from this
yearning, how it becomes the means for greater understanding
and insight about what our true self really is.

While erotic love is inherently self-regarding in its initiation—
that is, it seeks what is good for one's self—it is also inherently
other-regarding as it discovers how "each type of beauty is
incomplete in itself," J.M.E. Moravcsik points out. What begins as
"aesthetic appreciation turns into appreciation for moral qualities,
and that, in turn, is transformed into appreciation of the beauty of
abstract intellectual systems."[8] The desire for beauty leads to an
enlargement of the self by leading one to see how self-interest is
implicated in community interests. This is clearly implied in the
description of the beauty of the activities and laws at the upper
end of the erotic ascent in the *Symposium* (210c); and it is what the
Republic is about as well.[9]

For Socrates, at least as Plato presents him to us, this was not
merely a remote ideal. In the *Apology* and the *Crito* he has so
much identified himself with improving the laws and practices of
Athens that, even in the face of death, he will not separate himself
from them or give up his habit of questioning and examining
politically prominent figures. Caring for this kind of human
excellence is what he has spent his whole life doing. His self-interest
has become indistinguishable from the best interests of the city as
a whole. This is not only good, it is good in an eternal sense. Thus,

he goes to his death serene in the confidence that "no evil can happen to a good man."[10]

Love, therefore, is our "guide" through life. It shows us the way and leads us to what is next. It is the orientation of our desire. It is not "wholly other" than we are now, nor is it simply identical with what we are now. It is in between. Love leads us out of ourselves, disengages us from where we are, and takes us to what is new. It is like a light that illumines our path through all the confusing possibilities before us.

Ultimately this means that what we love is our self, our own unfulfilled self. What we desire in all our striving is our own eternal reality. Because of our contingency, this is what we lack. This is what we desire. This is why it "belongs" to us.

The true aim of erotic love is revealed in an even stronger light in the latter part of the *Symposium*. Just after Socrates concludes his speech, Alcibiades drunkenly bursts in upon the party. Young, aristocratic, and very handsome, he and Socrates already have quite a history and the ensuing banter presumes familiarity with the erotic gamesmanship between older and younger men that was typical of the time. Alcibiades begins his speech ostensibly in praise of Socrates as the embodiment of erotic love — not unlike the characterization of love just given by Diotima — but it turns into a bitter denunciation of the way Socrates has treated him and others. "He has deceived us all," complains Alcibiades (222b). Socrates presents himself as the lover but very quickly becomes the beloved rather than the lover. Socrates' well-known interest in attractive young men energizes his love of truth — the one passion that masters all other passions — but also awakens the young men to their own ignorance. Because Socrates exemplifies the autonomy and integrity that they lack, the pursuer instead becomes the pursued — a role reversal takes place. The renunciation of base pleasures in the the quest for truth turns the game of love around and enables Socrates to "master" Alcibiades' flattery and resist his seductive ploys. In book 4 of the *Republic* (443de), this ideal of "self-mastery" is celebrated as the epitome of the just life. Truth is power.[11]

Socrates' emotional involvement is always limited and under control, but when Alcibiades is instead ensnared by Socrates' inner beauty, the unhappy comparison makes him cry out, "my life isn't worth living" (216a). The excitement, new energy and sharpened perceptions move Socrates farther up the ladder of love, but

Alcibiades, even though he too may have benefited by a heightened understanding, nonetheless feels used because his mere physical good looks is not enough to hold Socrates' attention. Alcibiades' resentment of Socrates shows what happens when we fail to see the discipline in erotic love. The fact that he is drunk loosens his tongue enough to tell the harsh truth about Socrates (and about erotic love), but it does not enable him to see that his desire failed because it had become focused on sexual gratification rather than on the good. He does not see that sexual attraction is only the beginning of our erotic interest. If we are real lovers we desire the real beauty of our beloved, something beyond the fluctuations of appetites and sensual appearances. Erotic love seeks to disclose or engender what is truly desirable—that is, what is beautiful—about the other person. Socrates does not respond to Alcibiades' overtures because they are merely sexual and not truly erotic. As Socrates says to Alcibiades, "you offer me the merest appearance of beauty, and in return you want the thing itself, gold in exchange for bronze" (219a).

THE ROLE OF SEXUALITY

The coincidence of sexual desire and erotic love is why we typically regard them as synonymous. But sometimes Plato himself seems to be ambivalent about the relationship between them. In some texts he strongly implies that all bodily appetites are contrary to intellectual and spiritual development and must be overcome. In the *Phaedo*, for example, the body is the "prison-house of the soul" and indulgence in the pleasures of eating, drinking, and sex can only have a corrupting effect on the soul. The true lover of knowledge will seek to separate his mind from these sensual distractions in order to come closer to beauty and truth.[12]

In the *Republic* sex is acknowledged to have a certain utilitarian importance (procreation), but it is carefully regulated in the ideal society to restrict it to that function. Human nature is not defined biologically, but by the capacity to reason, and Plato argues that women are just as capable in this regard as men. "The only difference apparent between them is that the female bears and the male begets," he says, and "we shall not admit that this is a difference relevant to our purpose" (454e). The men and women who are to rule the ideal society (the Guardian class) shall be "lovers of being" (480a), not lovers of bodies. The "frenzy" of sexual activity is even disparaged as a distraction to the true love of beauty (403a).

In the *Phaedrus*, however, sexual desire and erotic love seem almost indistinguishable. The language used is the language of inflamed sensuality and Plato is surprisingly explicit in saying that this means "to see, to touch, to kiss, to lie down together" (255e). In contrast to the *Phaedo*, here Plato seems to think that bodily desire is a help, not a hindrance, to the acquisition of truth and beauty.

Moreover, there is no doubt that it is the love of two males that is being described in the *Phaedrus*. This is the case in the *Symposium* as well: nearly all the preliminary speakers, as well as Alcibiades, are quite overt in implying that this is what they are talking about. For whatever reasons, it is clear that what we call "homosexual" love was not only acceptable behavior in ancient Greece, but was even idealized, as can be seen in these two dialogues.[13] Michel Foucault observes, "The Greeks did not see love for one's own sex and love for the other sex as opposites, as two exclusive choices, two radically different types of behavior."[14] Typically, young men gave up their same-sex preferences when it came time to marry. But it was not the substitution of one appetite for another. The nature of desire was the same, regardless of the object it sought. However, even though men married women and had children, because women were restricted to the domestic scene and were not active in politics or business or warfare, they were not regarded as peers and hence not perceived as appropriate love-partners in the more elevated sense.

Plato was out of step with his times when he makes the point in the *Republic* that women could be the intellectual equals to men. Far more typical is his portrayal of Socrates' erotic interest in attractive young men, as in the beginning of *Charmides*. But the significance of this erotic by-play is the way it contextualizes the problem of the subsequent discussion about self-control and the search for knowledge. Socrates is not interested in young men as such but in the image of beauty that they bear. As Alcibiades notes ruefully, Socrates' well-known fascination with good-looking young men is actually only a game — "a game of irony" (216e).

For Plato the specific physical character or naturalistic origin of erotic love is not what is important, whether it be homosexual or heterosexual. (Remember that in the *Symposium* it is a woman who teaches Socrates about love.) What counts is whether it is powerful enough to engage the mind with a vision of beauty that will lift it beyond the level of physical passion. It is the shared vision of what is good and true and beautiful that truly unites lover and beloved, not the nature of their physical intercourse.

The term "Platonic love," which is usually taken to mean a nonsexual relationship, is thus somewhat misleading. While Plato clearly believes that the ultimate aim of love is beyond the sexual level, he is nonetheless quite insistent that it must begin where we are, with the love of some instance of physical beauty.

OUTCOMES

Erotic love is essentially energy. It is the most basic desire of the soul to overcome its contingency and unite with what is really real. In the *Phaedrus* it is described as a kind of "madness" (244–245) that Plato compares to a charioteer struggling to keep control over a bad horse, wild and fierce in its passion for the beloved, and a good horse, obedient and restrained in its approach. The charioteer, reason, has the vision of beauty but is overawed by it. It is the bad horse, barely under control, whose lustful energy drags them forward and forces them to approach the beloved (253–254). No such turbulent struggle is described in the *Symposium*. Here the contrary impulses of love are smoothly brought together in one continuous desire that ascends easily from physical to spiritual in uninterrupted development.

It would be hard to say which is the more accurate picture of human erotic experience. Perhaps this is why Plato gives us both. Sometimes love does indeed seem to be a mad passion in which we are driven to act in wildly uncharacteristic ways. It is exhilarating, often painful, and usually does not last very long, but we cannot deny that we see and feel differently as a result. But sometimes we are surprised to find how one desire can lead to another in a remarkably logical way. We become shrewd and calculating when we are led by desire. The white heat of passion prompts all sorts of strategies and maneuvers that would never occur to us otherwise.

The fact is, both dialogues suggest that reason and love work together—and they work together creatively. This is why Diotima reminds Socrates that the original meaning of the word "poetry" is "creativity." "Everything that is responsible for creating something out of nothing is a kind of poetry," she tells him. "That's also how it is with love" (205cd). Love in its very nature is poetic: it constantly seeks something other than what is—it seeks what is new and undisclosed. This is what makes erotic love so exciting. There is the continual emergence of what is new—in the other as desire illumines previously unnoticed aspects of the beloved, and in oneself as desire leads one to venture beyond previous limits. The erotic lover feels himself to be a new person because he has grown to find delight and appreciation in things he had not known before.

"All of us are pregnant," says Diotima to Socrates, "both in body and soul" and feel this "desire to give birth," that is, to bring ourselves forth, but "only in something beautiful," never in ugliness (206c). In the *Theaetetus* Socrates describes his role as that of a "midwife."[15] His function is to enable people to give birth to the truth within themselves, to bring it forth by dialectical examination. True learning is not putting things into people's heads but bringing to light and making coherent their own intuitions of what is good and true and beautiful. Love is the relation that brings these dim intuitions out of our dark interiors into the light of day where their truth and consistency can be tested and examined. Thus, in love do we give birth to ourselves.[16]

However, while erotic love does indeed draw the self out of its isolation and leads it to the formation of practices (dialogue, politics) and principles (science, art) that constitute the cement of social life, it is arguable whether it has solved the problem of loneliness. Both Plato's dialogues on love show this. At the end of the *Symposium*, after exhausting the conversation of its possibilities, Socrates goes off *alone* at dawn to begin his day. At the end of the *Phaedrus*, the prayer that Socrates makes to the god Pan is a prayer of *individual* aspiration: "Grant me to be beautiful within ..."(279c). The "other" that erotic love seeks is clearly not other people as such, but a quality or standard of excellence for oneself.

ASSESSMENT

What can we expect of erotic love?

First and foremost erotic love can be expected to pursue what is interesting. Our sense of what we lack is its own authority.

Attempts at persuasion or dissuasion are usually pointless. We want what we want. We may eventually come to see a desire as unworthy, but it will continue to look beautiful to us until we have it. The logic of erotic love leads to discovery, newness, growth, and development. This is why anticipation, yearning, striving are often far more exciting than possessing. Love understood in this way is actually defeated by success. What is won is always lost, Diotima says about love.[17]

To have something is no longer to desire it. A new focus of desire is then necessary and the serious lover learns fairly soon that mere novelty is not enough. The sameness and similarities of new relationships, new objects of desire, become apparent—and this is boring. A lover is compelled by the restlessness of desire to raise his or her sights and become more demanding, more inventive, more perceptive. But of course nothing in the world could possibly meet these increasingly rigorous expectations. This kind of lover is in the relentless pursuit of something that is truly otherworldly.

Such a lover is a perfectionist, although he would not claim to know what "perfect" is. This would always be a little beyond him, something that he was only approaching asymptotically. He would know that he always had more to learn and that what he already knew was of small account. Nonetheless he would be sensitive to even the most partial appearances of beauty, truth, and goodness in the world.

What we cannot expect of erotic love is stability and fidelity, at least not with respect to persons or objects. There is, to be sure, a certain consistency in the ideals to which it is committed, but these transcend individuals. No single relationship could possibly bear the weight of erotic demand. This kind of love is as destructive of relationships as it is creative.

Ironically, however, while erotic love may not contribute to stable personal relationships, it could lead to lifelong dedication to certain professions or institutions or artistic endeavors. Institutions are of course as limited and fallible as anything else in the world, but their standards and goals are often otherworldly in their ideality. It is not surprising, then, that Plato says the upper reaches of love's aim will be found "in activities and laws" and in "beautiful ideas and theories" (210cd). All of one's energies can be absorbed in striving for beauty of this kind and its realizations have at least a degree of objectivity and permanence. Mere physical beauty is "a thing of no importance" and the failures of one's personal life may not seem too high a price to pay.

FURTHER READING

There are many good translations of Plato's *Symposium*. One of the best, by Alexander Nehamas and Paul Woodruff (Indianapolis: Hackett Publishing Co., 1989), is the one used in this discussion. The Introduction, Notes, and Bibliography are particularly helpful. Another very readable translation is by W. Hamilton (Harmondsworth: Penguin Books, 1951).

Plato's *Phaedrus* is available in a good translation by W. C. Helmbold and W. G. Rabinowitz (Indianapolis: Library of Liberal Arts, Bobbs-Merrill Co., 1956).

Plato's major work, *The Republic*, is available in a good translation by Desmond Lee, second edition, revised, (Harmondsworth: Penguin Books, 1974).

The secondary literature on Plato is immense. W.K.C. Guthrie's *The Greek Philosophers – From Thales to Aristotle* (New York: Harper Torchbook , Harper & Row, 1960) is helpful for beginners to establish the historical context and major themes of Plato's dialogues as well as Aristotle's work, and has suggestions for further reading.

Michel Foucault's *The History of Sexuality*, vol. 2, *The Use of Pleasure*, trans., Robert Hurley (New York: Vintage Books, Random House, 1986) shows how the social values of ancient Greece shaped the idea of love. See Part 5, "True Love," on Plato's *Symposium*.

Two fine scholarly studies on Plato are Thomas Gould, *Platonic Love* (Glencoe: Free Press, 1963) and A. W. Price, *Love and Friendship in Plato and Aristotle* (Oxford: Clarendon Press, 1989).

Luce Irigaray (see chapter 7 of this book) offers a woman's appraisal of Diotima's voice in Plato's *Symposium* in the first chapter of *An Ethics of Sexual Difference*, translated by Carolyn Burke and Gillian C. Gill (Ithaca: Cornell University Press, 1993).

The Nature of Love – Plato to Luther by Irving Singer (New York: Random House, 1966) is an informative and insightful history of the notion of love. This volume focuses mainly on Platonic and Christian contributions.

Eros, Agape and Philia – Readings in the Philosophy of Love, edited by Alan Soble (New York: Paragon House, 1989) is a useful collection of essays, some of which are important scholarly contributions, and includes many references for further study.

NOTES

1. Plato, *Symposium*, trans. A. Nehamas and P. Woodruff (Indianapolis: Hackett Publishing Co., 1989), 178c, p. 9.

2. Plato, *Phaedrus*, trans. W. C. Helmbold and W. G. Rabinowitz (Indianapolis: Library of Liberal Arts, Bobbs-Merrill Co., 1956), 250e, p. 34.

3. Irving Singer, *The Nature of Love — Plato to Luther* (New York: Random House, 1966), p. 88.

4. Iris Murdoch, *Metaphysics as a Guide to Morals* (New York: Allen Lane/Penguin Press, 1992), p. 405.

5. "The good, then, is the end of all endeavor, the object on which every heart is set." Plato, *The Republic*, trans. Desmond Lee, 2nd ed., rev. (New York: Penguin Books, 1974), bk. 6, 505d, p. 304.

6. Plato, *Lysis, Socratic Discourses by Plato and Xenophon*, trans. J. Wright (New York: Everyman's Library, 1910), 219d, 221e.

7. L. A. Kosman, "Platonic Love," in *Facets of Plato's Philosophy*, ed. W.H. Werkmeister (Assen, Amsterdam: Van Gorcum 1976), p. 60.

8. J.M.E. Moravcsik, "Reason and Eros in the 'Ascent' — Passage of the Symposium," in *Essays in Ancient Greek Philosophy*, ed. John P. Anton with George L. Kustas (Albany: SUNY, 1971), pp. 288, 289.

9. *Republic*, bk. 3, 412d, 420, and bk. 5, 474c.

10. Plato, *Euthyphro, Apology, Crito*, trans. F. J. Church (Indianapolis: Library of Liberal Arts, Bobbs-Merrill Co., 1956), XVII 30–31, pp. 36–37.

11. "Into the lover's game where different dominations confronted one another (that of the lover seeking to get control of the beloved, that of the beloved seeking to escape, and seeking, by means of his resistance, to enslave the lover), Socrates introduces another type of domination: that which is exercised by the master of truth and for which he is qualified by the dominion he exercises over himself." Michel Foucault, *The History of Sexuality*, vol. 2, *The Use of Pleasure*, trans. Robert Hurley (New York: Vintage Books, Random House, 1986), p. 242.

12. Plato, *Phaedo*, trans. F. J. Church (Indianapolis: Library of Liberal Arts, Bobbs-Merrill Publishing Co., 1951), 66–67, pp. 11–12.

13. A relation between an adult male and an adolescent boy, an *erastes* (lover) and an *eromenes* (beloved), was not uncommon. See K. J. Dover, *Greek Homosexuality* (New York: Random House, 1978).

14. Michel Foucault, *The History of Sexuality*, vol. 2, *The Use of Pleasure*, trans. Robert Hurley (New York: Vintage Books, Random House, 1986), p. 187. As Foucault goes on to point out, the "moral" question was not so much the gender of one's erotic object, but whether one was the dominant or submissive partner. For a free man to be an object of pleasure for another was

clearly unacceptable. In other words, the power relation defined its moral status. See pp. 220–225.

15. Plato, *Theatetus*, trans. F. M. Cornford (Indianapolis: Library of Liberal Arts, Bobbs-Merrill Publishing Co.), 149–150, pp. 24–26.

16. Kosman, "Platonic Love," pp. 61, 62–65.

17. "anything he finds his way to always slips away." Plato, *Symposium*, 203e, p. 49.

Chapter 3
℘

CHRISTIAN LOVE: GENESIS 1 TO I CORINTHIANS 13

To have joy in another is love.

—Karl Barth

Christian love is difficult to understand because it involves something more than human relationships. Another factor, God, has to be considered, not just as an addition to the human equation, but as the very basis of human relationships. The love of God not only takes precedence over finding oneself in another, but fundamentally alters both the nature of the self and the other.

This begs the question, of course, as to who or what God is or why human affairs should require this kind of outside interference, but this would be a much larger inquiry than can be undertaken here. The task of this chapter is to identify what is distinctive about Christian love, and to do this I propose a fresh look at some of the most important messages in the Bible. However, there are many texts within the Bible (sixty-six books in the Old and New Testaments) and many different communities—Jewish as well as Christian—that have interpreted those texts. I cannot, therefore, represent this discussion as authoritative but only as my attempt to understand the meaning of these biblical messages for the Christian concept of love. To focus on some texts while ignoring others admittedly does not do justice to the rich diversity of biblical materials and also runs the risk of making the Bible appear more systematic than it really is. I think the risk is worth taking, however, in order to highlight what seems to be so distinctive about the notion of Christian love as expressed by biblical writers.

The Christian concept of love is unique because it is tied to the affirmation of God's transcendence over nature and history. Despite the great variety of voices and literary forms in the Bible, its one persistent theme is that all our relationships to each other as well as our relation to nature only make sense in relation to God, who is beyond both nature and man. "In the beginning, God" are the very first words of the first book, Genesis. God's dominion over nature is of course what the creation story is all about, but it is also reasserted in the promise made to Abraham that he and his descendants will be a great nation and its subsequent renewal in the covenant with Israel. And this is not just an Old Testament story. All the New Testament materials not only re-echo this affirmation, but declare that it has been most dramatically demonstrated in the triumph of Jesus as the Christ over nature's ultimate limit—death itself, which the apostle Paul calls "the last enemy" to be overcome.[1]

Whatever else God is, therefore, it is clear that God is not to be understood as something "natural." In the book of Genesis God brings nature into being, out of the void. In a series of creative acts, light and the heavens and the waters and the earth and all the creatures of the earth are brought forth. God is clearly prior to nature and above it. He is not a part of nature but transcends it.

The human story is inextricably tied up with this relation to an "other" that is never defined or explained, only acknowledged. The stories of the promise to Abraham, the covenant with Israel, and the ups and downs of its subsequent history all show God's initiative and continuing transcendence. The Bible simply takes it as given that humankind exists in relation to God—to an "other" that is at once wholly unlike anything human and yet a presence that has human characteristics such as anger (Judges 2:12) and sorrow (Genesis 6:6). But when Moses seeks to know who calls him into action, he is only told, "I am who I am" (Exodus 3:14).

Not to be missed in this biblical picture, moreover, is the portrayal of human beings as being capable of standing in a relationship with God. That is, humankind may be creatures just like everything else in nature, but they are also "godlike" in a very special way. Man is made, says the book of Genesis, in the "image of God." What does this mean? The text makes it clear: man is to "have dominion over the fish of the sea, and over the birds of the air, and over the cattle, and over all the earth, and over every creeping thing that creeps upon the earth" (Genesis 1:26). In other words, man is "godlike" in his transcendence over nature.

Man is like all the rest of nature in his limitations, his physical characteristics, and his temporality. He is born and he dies. But unlike the rest of nature he has the capacity to dominate it, to manipulate it, to make it serve his own purposes, and in some instances, to overcome it entirely. For example, smallpox, a terrible disease that once annihilated whole populations and disfigured countless generations, has been wiped from the face of the earth by human ingenuity.

Even more striking are the ways in which this godlike power enables man to act in a manner that seems to surpass his own nature. Nobody is surprised when someone acts to pursue his own interests or defends himself from attack or seeks to save his own life. This is natural, we say. But there are times when we find someone actually giving up his own interest or even going so far as to sacrifice his life for another. We may regard such astonishing acts as admirable or as foolish but they nonetheless are evidence of this godlike ability to transcend what is "natural" and to do things that are wholly unexpected or unnecessary.

Almost any natural necessity can be denied: to the need for food we can fast, to the need for sex we can be celibate, to the need for society we can be hermits. Logical necessity is no more compelling: we can turn deaf ears to any reasoning, to any logical arguments, and act absolutely arbitrarily. This does not mean that we can do anything we want to do; we are after all limited, determinate beings like everything else in the world. But our dominion over nature and reason shows that we are fundamentally unlike anything else in the world. There is something open and indeterminate in all human experience, and this means that how we love is similarly open and undetermined.

A brief comparison with Plato's erotic love shows how different the biblical picture of human nature is. Erotic love is based on the unfolding logic of human need — we love what we lack. Christian love, however, originates in a presence within human experience, unbidden and undefined, that transcends the logic of nature and the calculation of self-interest. The openness thus created is what

sets the stage for the human drama portrayed in the narratives
and poetry of the Old Testament as well as the Gospels and letters
of the New Testament.

THE DEFINING RELATION

What establishes this openness in human beings? The Bible is
unequivocal in stating that this sovereignty over things in the world
is "the image of God" — that human freedom is the result of our
relation to the absolute freedom of God. It is a "given" of the
human condition — something we ourselves did not make nor can
we fully account for it. Obviously human freedom could not arise
out of our relation to nature since everything in nature is determined
by necessity of some kind. There is no freedom in nature. It cannot
act arbitrarily or illogically but only according to some determined
principle. Natural law, we call it. Only in relation to that which is
wholly other than nature, to God, do we find our own freedom.
God's transcendence is the guarantee of our own transcendence.

This then is the defining relation: to the extent that we are
faithful to this absolute otherness of God — his sovereignty over
things in the world — to that extent are we human and able to
maintain our freedom. To the extent that we relinquish this
commitment we see ourselves and others as determinate objects,
like anything else in nature, and surrender our freedom. Instead
of acting out of godlike freedom, we act out of natural need.

To be made in the "image of God" means that the preeminent
characteristic of the self is not how it is constituted by natural or
historical forces, but is rather its power to make relationships that
overcome such limitations. Things like ethnic origin, gender roles,
or economic status need not determine my relationships with
others. These walls come down. I am "open" to other possibilities.
Love is precisely this freedom for our fellow human beings, for the
other person. This openness is the result of our relation to God's
absolute transcendence. To love God is to place this relation before
anything else. The only "other" in which we can find what is like
ourselves is the divine "Other."

The significance of Jesus as the Christ is that he is the full
embodiment of the "image of God" in man. His life demonstrates
the presence of transcendence in his lack of both fear and desire,
in his unwillingness to condemn or approve, in his nonresistance

to evil. In a sense, he is "beyond" all of these things; he has no interests to advance or defend other than the Kingdom of God. The Gospels present Jesus as a miracle worker who comes preaching the Kingdom of God. But the real miracle is his demonstration of what this means: a freedom not only from the old Jewish law, but from every conventional notion of human value—as the Sermon on the Mount reveals (Matthew 5-7). To receive the Kingdom of God like a child (Mark 10:13-16) is to display the innocent fearlessness of the freedom that is given when God is truly the one in whom one finds himself.

But we dare not see what Jesus is talking about simply as an extension or enhancement of ordinary human affections. There is an element of detachment, bordering on indifference, in this kind of godlike caring. It is a dispassionate love that in fact can be shockingly harsh: "He who loves father or mother more than me is not worthy of me," says Jesus, "and he who loves son or daughter more than me is not worthy of me"(Matthew 10:37). These words echo the story in Genesis 22, when Abraham is told to take Isaac— "your only son, whom you love" —up to Mt. Moriah for sacrifice. The story leaves no doubt as to the exclusivity of the God-relation. Abraham gets Isaac back, but as a *gift*, not as a possession. Love based on the God-relation bluntly sets aside any sentimental understanding of love from a natural point of view. Love cuts into love, Paul Tillich reminds us. Love requires both self-acceptance and the acceptance of the other's separateness, however painful that might be.[2]

This new model of what it means to live in the presence of transcendence strongly enhances my sense of individuality, since my sense of self is undetermined by anything other than my relation to God. But it also somewhat distances my relations to others since there could be no other person in whom I could find the full range of my freedom. In any serious relationship, instead of finding myself in the other, sooner or later I come up against the limitations of the other's freedom—suspicion, misunderstanding, resentment. What Christians mean by love, therefore, always requires "God as the middle term," as Kierkegaard would say.[3] Only the fact that I and the other person are mutually related to God's transcendence enables us to overcome one another's limitations.

Thus my relation to another is not based on what I need or on what qualities the beloved has. "Loving means neither esteeming, nor admiring nor revering," declares Karl Barth. "Loving means simply accepting the other in his place and in his way of life exactly as he is."[4] In contrast to erotic love, freedom, not desire, is at the heart of the matter. Love in this sense is the gift of what the self is—freedom. To stand in a loving relation with another person is to give what I have been given. In a paradoxical way the most unique act of the self is to be self*less*. The relationship to God— absolute transcendence—not only guarantees my freedom but enables me to accept the limitations of others as well as to respect the dignity of their freedom, no matter how it affects me.

"An obsessed egoist, almost everyone sometimes," says Iris Murdoch, "destroys the space and air round about him and is uncomfortable to be with." Whereas, she continues, "an unselfish person enlarges the space and the world."[5] This "sense of the 'space' of others" creates an atmosphere in which neither desire nor fear plays a role. Others are "given their rights," as it were. If this kind of love seeks anything, it is only to want others to stand in the same relation to transcendence as I do, so as to open up the space in which we live.

What kind of relationship does this create? To love someone in this way does not mean that I belong to him or her or that he or she belongs to me, but rather that we both depend on something that we could not give ourselves—freedom. What holds us together is this mutual acknowledgment. This is what the community of faith is. But this acknowledgment is more than mere reverence, it is empowering. This is what enables us to give up certain expectations of the other that may have been oppressive; it is what enables us to let go of suspicions of the other that may have been crippling. In a word, the presence of this freedom is the experience of forgiveness.

Without being forgiven and forgiving others we would be helplessly chained to our former actions, actions for which we may well be responsible but which had consequences we did not intend or could not have expected. To assert this transcendence over past actions is a godlike power. Thus Jesus amazes people with the authority he demonstrates when he forgives sins and the scribes charge him with blasphemy: "Who can forgive sins but God alone?" (Mark 2:7).

To be human is to act—to make things happen in word and deed—but no one can foresee the outcome of one's words or actions. Once they are done we cannot take them back. Actions set events in motion that have a continuity and force of their own — and they are irreversible. One can hardly overestimate the importance of being able to break out of the constraints of the past and make a new departure. All faith and hope in the future spring from our ability to reconceive what is "normal" and "natural." The presence of transcendence opens the world to new possibilities. No one has shown more insightfully how this release from the past and the power to act anew are rooted in Christian teaching than the philosopher, Hannah Arendt. "The discoverer of the role of forgiveness in human affairs," she says, "was Jesus of Nazareth."[6]

"Without being forgiven," she points out, without being "released from the consequences of what we have done, our capacity to act would be confined to one single deed from which we could never recover. We would remain victims of its consequences forever."[7] We would be trapped by inexorable fatality. Forgiveness introduces something new into human experience. Because of the presence of freedom we are capable of responses that do not merely re-act but act anew and unexpectedly. Forgiveness is not contained in the original action, as is vengeance. It is new. "Forgiving," says Arendt, "is the only reaction which does not merely re-act but acts anew and unexpectedly, unconditioned by the act which provoked it and therefore freeing from its consequences both the one who forgives and the one who is forgiven."[8]

While forgiveness sets us free from the bondage of the past, our ability to make promises overcomes the uncertainties of the future. Again, it is the gift of transcendence that enables us to commit ourselves beyond the immediate moment to future contingencies. We promise to keep a date, we promise to repay a loan, we promise to be loyal. By projecting our freedom over time we create an island of stability in a sea of uncertainty. Since promises are never made in isolation but to others, they are how loving relationships and communities are established. What sustains them is no natural or logical necessity, but only the power of freedom. That such promises often fail should therefore be no surprise, and once again, only forgiveness can reinstate them.

No wonder then that the writer of the first letter of John in the latter part of the New Testament says that "he who does not love remains in death" (I John 3:14). Would life be truly human without giving, forgiving, and promising? Abiding human relationships are only possible because of the almost miraculous transcendence that lifts us above our natural limits, our guilty past, and our uncertain future. In the fullest sense this is what human life is and this is why the God-relation is the defining relation: "He who does not love does not know God, for God is love" (I John 4:8). Whatever else the writer of I John means, he means at least this.

THE ROLE OF REASON

Reason shows how things are alike and how they differ and how to find identity even in differences. Plato showed us how love and reason collaborate to lead us to this kind of logical understanding.

Is there anything comparable in the biblical view? Yes, I think there is, but to see it we have to shift from the idea of erotic love to the very different notion of love as the presence of transcendence that I have just sketched out.

The Bible is largely a book of stories. It does not attempt to explain human experience in terms of natural characteristics or logical principles. There is no drama, no "story," in an outcome already determined. If it is man's relation to transcendent freedom that is definitive, then the outcome is always uncertain and undetermined. One can only talk about how that freedom is revealed in one's actions — one's history. The reason why human history is never quite repeatable (and why every generation must rewrite its history) is that such accounts reveal this openness in human experience. The presence of freedom (or the absence of natural determinism) means that we are never certain of the outcome. We do not know what Pharaoh will do when confronted by Moses' demand to let his people go, we do not know what King David will do about the treachery of his son, Absalom, and we do not even know what Jesus will do in the dark night of Gethsemane.

The Bible therefore is not merely a form of primitive understanding or a quaint collection of prescientific myths and legends. There is an intrinsic relation between its narrative form and the uncertain drama between God and man which is essential to human freedom. Hence, the thread that ties much of the Old Testament together is the promise that God makes to Abraham

(Genesis 12) that he and his descendants will be a great nation. The outcome was uncertain then and still is — and what does "great" mean? Although this promise is never explained and never justified, all the subsequent inheritors of that promise identify themselves in terms of that relationship. That is, they understand who they are by an act of freedom that they receive and to which they respond. That they are nearly always unfaithful is certainly no surprise; what is significant is that the promise is repeatedly renewed and the history of Israel is the story of this repeated renewal.

Explanation here does not consist of generalizations about a body of facts or deductions from known principles. It is rather a kind of historical understanding that relies instead on memory and hope — memory of a promise made and hope of its future fulfillment. Particular events and individual persons are made significant by their relation to the community that bears these memories and hopes.

The gift of freedom and the recurring call to be faithful to that freedom are taken by Old Testament writers to be evidence of God's love for his people. The most dramatic example is the deliverance from bondage in Egypt, followed by the giving of the law. God's relation to his people is manifested first in freedom and then in the law. In the Old Testament the law is the specification of responsibility that freedom makes possible, whereas in the New Testament the law is superseded by radical freedom embodied in the figure of Jesus as the Christ. In instance after instance Jesus shows that the reach of freedom cannot be limited to the law: "You have heard that it was said, 'An eye for an eye and a tooth for a tooth' but I say to you, do not resist one who is evil" (Matthew 5:38) — nor even to natural relationships: "Who is my mother, and who are my brothers?" (Matthew 12:48).

In other words, this new kind of love makes a shambles of all ordinary relationships and defies ordinary rationality. Because of the freedom man has access to, there is no limit to what he may do — even to the point of sacrificing his own life. When Jesus goes to the cross, he demonstrates this freedom to the fullest. As the fullest act of selflessness his deed does not change the fact that men die, but it does change its significance. In the new era that he inaugurates, the gift of self will define what it means to be human, not the brute facticity of death.

THE ROLE OF SEXUALITY

As a natural function it is obvious that sexuality is not going to play a decisive role in Christian love, although in and of itself there is nothing wrong with it. As the first chapter of Genesis repeatedly declares, everything in God's creation is good. The question, however, is not whether sex is good or bad; the question is one of sovereignty. Do a man's actions demonstrate his freedom over nature or that he is a function of nature? Jesus' comments make it very clear that man's dominion over nature may require drastic steps — cutting off a hand or a foot or plucking out an eye, if necessary (Matthew 18:8-9), or even going so far as making oneself a eunuch (Matthew 19:12).

The point here is that it is not our physical natures but our capacity for entering into relationships, our capacity for promising and forgiving, that defines our humanity. Given that power of transcendence, sexuality could well perform a sacramental function: that is, it could be a means by which freedom is made present to another person. This is why marriage is a Christian sacrament; the promises that a man and a woman make to each other liberate them from the natural force of sexual need by giving themselves to each other, but they could also have the paradoxical effect of liberating them from the need for sex altogether. What makes the marriage is the promising and the forgiving, not sex.

But sexuality has long been a problem in the Christian tradition, and it appears early, in the letters of the apostle Paul who openly confesses his problems with "living in the flesh" (Romans 7:5) — that is, like Plato he seems to blame his body for his problems: "For I know that nothing good dwells within me, that is, within my flesh. I can will what is right but I cannot do it. For I do not do the good that I want, but the evil I do not want is what I do." There is, he says, "a law of sin which dwells in my members" that is "at war with the law of my mind" (Romans 7:18-19, 23).

The rather obvious sexual overtones in Paul's preoccupation with personal purity sound rather strident in contrast to the more open and confident mood of the Gospels' proclamation of the Kingdom of God. Paul's letters are much more passionate and moralistic. At his best, however, he understands that the problem is not the dualistic struggle of soul against body, but one of freedom.

Even in the passage just quoted he rejoices that he has been "set free" from the law of sin and death (Romans 8:2).

In other letters he declares further that because God was in Christ he sees that he is now "a new creation" (II Corinthians 5:17) and has a "new nature" (Colossians 3:10) that is liberated from bondage to the flesh. Not surprisingly, he finds the origin of this freedom in the promise given to Abraham and the giving of the law that established Israel's identity in that relationship. The advent of Christ, however, has brought a new understanding of this relationship: "There is neither Jew nor Greek, there is neither slave nor free, there is neither male nor female; for you are all one in Christ Jesus" (Galatians 3:28). Not only is sexuality transcended but so is everything else. "For freedom Christ has set us free; stand fast therefore, and do not submit again to a yoke of slavery" (Galatians 5:1). The full thrust of what Paul means becomes apparent when he goes so far as to say that this new relation constitutes "adoption as sons" — sons of God (Galatians 4:5-7).

One might think that this startling language is mere rhetorical exaggeration on Paul's part were it not for the fact that human divinization is also a constant theme of the gospel of John (17:21, for example) and is also affirmed by 2 Peter (1:4). Moreover, the early church fathers seem to have taken the deification of man quite seriously. Athanasius, for example, declared in the fourth century that "God became man that man might be made god," and, significantly, both he and Clement of Alexandria link man's divinization with the power of forgiveness.[9]

The apostle Paul's tendency to identify one's physical (that is, sexual) nature with sin is the beginning of a long history of Christian puritanism and obsession with personal purity. It was strongly reinforced in the fourth century by Augustine, whose conversion to Christianity is closely linked to his struggles with sexuality. He prays to God for chastity, "but not yet," he confesses, because his lusts have too strong a grip on him.[10] When he later becomes a bishop, Augustine identifies his sexual problem with that of the whole human race and traces it all the way back to the "original sin" of Adam and Eve's sexuality. By such reasoning Augustine seeks to show that sin is inescapable in the human condition and that freedom is impossible.[11] As a result, conservative Christian theologies in the Western tradition have stressed human unworthiness and total dependence on God for salvation.[12] Sex and sin have been virtually synonymous ever since, one of the unfortunate legacies of Augustinian theology.[13]

In contrast to the Latin tradition represented by Augustine, we should take note of another fourth-century church father, Gregory of Nyssa, from the Eastern (Greek) Christian tradition. Like Athanasius and Clement of Alexandria, Gregory strongly links divinization with human freedom. A recent study by Verna Harrison concludes that for Gregory "both God and the human person are equally free of external necessity in their choices, and that the freedom of each is equally self-initiating in its activity." Thus, "self-determination is equal to God," Gregory boldly declares.[14] Man has the status of royalty because he has been made in "the living image of the King of all," set to rule over the world. As if in reply to Augustine, Gregory asks, "How can that nature which is under a yoke and bondage to any kind of necessity be called a Master Being?"[15] Since freedom is an attribute of God, the image of God in man must also be characterized by this same freedom, including the power of self-determination: "we are in some manner our own parents, giving birth to ourselves by our own free choice."[16] Self-mastery is to Gregory the highest form of freedom. The problems with our passions, therefore, are not due to bodily enslavement, but to a surrender of dominion, and even then the power of choice is still with us and can be reasserted. According to Gregory, the image of God in man means that every choice is a new initiative and not bound by any necessity to sin. No matter how corrupt we become, the power of self-determination remains intact.

OUTCOMES

It is clear, then, that Christian love must be understood in terms of man's extraordinary sovereignty over nature, over law, and even over death itself. Paul's famous description of love in chapter 13 of his letter to the Corinthians is preliminary to his declaration in chapter 15 that "the last enemy to be destroyed is death" (I Corinthians 15:26). The utter selflessness of what he says about love in chapter 13, therefore, must be understood in the context of this radical freedom from the ordinary limitations of human nature. He makes it clear that this is not something marginal; it is definitive: "If I speak in the tongues of men and of angels...if I have prophetic powers and understand all mysteries...if I have all faith...if I give away all that I have, and if I deliver my body to be burned, but have not love, I gain nothing."

He then follows by describing love as wholly without self-regarding concern: "Love is patient and kind...not jealous or boastful...not arrogant or rude...does not insist on its own way...is not irritable or resentful." This kind of love, in other words, is free from possessiveness, either of the other or of oneself. I can act freely, without either envy or resentment. I can cherish the freedom of the other because my own freedom is not in doubt.

Most important is Paul's conclusion that "love bears all things, hopes all things, endures all things. Love never ends." That is, it transcends. Because it is possessed by nothing it can reach beyond everything. Because it is tied to no natural or temporal state it is limitless in what it can do. "So faith, hope, love abide, these three; but the greatest of these is love."

Let us be very forthright and say that, as lovely as it sounds, what Paul describes is quite impossible for any human being to do. It is impossible to be human and be so totally detached from the very means by which we express our freedom. But on the other hand, it is impossible to be human if we are *not* detached from them. If we are possessed by our things or our projects—*our* way of doing things—we become captive to them. We become things ourselves if we lose our sovereignty. We cannot act, and we certainly cannot love.

The great confusion in discussions of Christian love takes place when we ignore this paradox. To assume that the transforming effects of love can be brought about by making them into a code of behavior is to miss the point of transcendence. Perhaps the account of love in I Corinthians 13 (and Romans 12 and Matthew 5) should not be taken so much as a moral imperative—what we *ought* to do—but rather as a description of *what actually happens* when we are being most human, when we are being most free. No human relationship can in fact be sustained without relying upon promises and acts of giving and forgiving that are in themselves unmerited. This is why every enduring human relationship is something of a mystery; it cannot quite be accounted for in terms of the facts. Love only "abides" when it is unaccountable—an act of pure godlike freedom. This is what Christians call "grace."

The danger in the Christian idea of love occurs when an aspiration *for* transcendence displaces the gift *of* transcendence. The inevitable temptation is to try to guarantee the presence of this "givenness" by stipulating certain conditions for it—to pull heaven down to earth, as it were. Instead of "resist not evil," which is an implicit affirmation that God's transcendence will prevail, specific evils are identified and condemned. Life is divided into moral and immoral, pure and impure; and transcendence (or holiness) is said to be present only when certain rules are observed. Of course, regulation and denial do not bring about transcendence. Selflessness cannot be mandated, but only given in response to what has been given.

The step from the acknowledgment of transcendence to the installation of the so-called rule of God does not seem to be a very big one, but it is a step that inverts the Christian idea of love from self-giving to self-achievement. In a way, it almost becomes a form of erotic striving. By not conforming to the world in certain designated ways, say, by rules of celibacy or chastity, it is assumed that transformation can be *made* to happen. If anything, the opposite is what takes place. Instead of self-giving, love becomes a kind of moralism, or, even worse, a repressive authoritarianism. Nothing denies the gift of transcendence more than the claim of divine authority. Pascal once observed, "Man is neither an angel nor a beast, but unfortunately when he tries to become an angel he becomes a beast."[17] To be simply a human being, made in the image of God, appears to be very difficult to do.

It seems odd that the notion of love as transcendent freedom should have originated in a people whose history is so provincial, so marginal to the rise and fall of great empires. And yet it is Israel's memory of liberation and its people's struggles to live according to their covenant of freedom that is at the heart of the modern idea of freedom. In appropriating this memory the early Christians understood it to be the promise that was fulfilled in Jesus as the Christ—a promise of life fulfilled in the Resurrection. So contrary to common sense was this that even the apostle Paul called it "folly" (I Corinthians 1:27), yet within several hundred years it became the orthodoxy of empire. To be sure, the Christian idea was often misunderstood and even more often subverted to serve the purposes of political power, but through it all certain key principles have persisted.

First is human freedom. If our relation to transcendence is what makes us human, then that is inextinguishable. No government or ruling power can deprive a person of his essential liberty. He can be made to suffer, he can be put in jail, he can have his life taken from him—but no one can take from him his capacity to defy every limit put before him. Human beings cannot be treated as things, as objects to be manipulated or disposed of.

Second is human uniqueness. If our relation to transcendence is what makes us human, then what each person does within that relation is his own, quite apart from his social context. His character is revealed in what he does with his sovereignty over himself. Each person is important because of the individual significance of his life.

Third is human equality. According to nature we differ in all kinds of ways—physical size, gender, race, intelligence, skills—as well as social status and wealth, but everyone is in the same position before God. The notion of human equality is based on our access to absolute transcendence. Every man is made "in the image of God." Every man is in the same position of relying upon a freedom that he did not give himself.

Simply to state these principles is to recognize immediately the core of modern moral consciousness. To argue against "liberty and equality for all" would be uphill work, indeed. That this moral vision should have had its origin in ancient tribal religious presumptions seems one of history's strangest ironies. The great work of the apostle Paul was to lift the identity of "the people of God" out of its Jewish ethnic context and place it within the new community of those who recognized Christ as Lord. In so doing the Christian community universalized the promise to Israel to mean God's love for all mankind and thereby set a standard of freedom that the church itself has had trouble living up to.[18]

However, despite its approval of both slavery and empire, despite its corruption and fragmentation, despite its inquisitions and persecution of dissent, the Christian community has carried along the essential idea of man's relation to a transcendent "other" that guarantees his freedom. What has happened in modern times, of course, is that this idea, in turn, has been lifted out of its Christian context and, together with the classical Greek idea of democracy, has become part of the unchallenged moral consciousness of the Western world. The transforming power of this idea in the world at large should not be underestimated. One cannot talk about love apart from its implications for justice. "Justice is immanent in love," Paul Tillich noted.[19] In the United States it was the black churches of the South that were the vanguard in bringing an end to racial segregation and oppression, and they did this through their willingness to nonviolently accept suffering even to the point of death for some, including their leader, Martin Luther King, Jr. In Poland it was the Roman Catholic church that formed the rallying point for the Polish people in their defiance of Soviet communism and finally led to the emergence of Solidarity and the reappearance of political freedom in Eastern Europe.

The question is, can this generalized notion of freedom exist apart from the transcendent relation that makes it possible? Or, to put it in religious language, can human beings love one another without loving God? Christians would say that this is not possible. The ability to live with one's own freedom and to accept the freedom of others depends upon the acknowledgment of its "givenness," that it is God's grace. Without this recognition and acceptance, freedom instead becomes anxiety, meaninglessness, and uncertainty; and in relation to others it becomes either tyranny or manipulation—the regard of others as objects to serve one's own purposes. Only a promising and forgiving community can sustain the memory and the hope that the presence of freedom is not made with human hands.

ASSESSMENT

What can we expect of Christian love?

One of the hardest things in the world to do is to treat another person as a human being. As strange as this sounds it seems nevertheless to be the case that a cherished relationship tempts us to either idealize the other person or to dehumanize him or her. That is, we either elevate the other to the level of the divine or we diminish him or her to the level of an object. We either expect too much or too little. To respect the dignity of the other's intrinsic freedom at the same time that we accept the frailty of his or her limitations requires an almost impossible combination of self-assurance and sensitivity. This is what we can expect of Christian love. It goes without saying that this is rarely experienced, but it is also true that life would not be worth living without some experience of it.

Given this lofty standard of love, why have Christians turned in such a miserably poor performance over the centuries? Contrary to what they profess, they have reviled, shunned, tortured, and killed one another, not to mention nonbelievers, all in the name of Christ—in the name of love.

The answer, I think, is that Christian love is indeed the hardest thing in the world to do. Radical freedom is also radical insecurity. There has to be some recognizable way of identifying our relation to transcendence—some doctrine, some ritual, some moral code that can provide a certain link. But of course no such link can contain the transcendence toward which it points. And so Christians in the eighth century wantonly destroyed images of Christ as idolatrous, and in the sixteenth century Martin Luther defied the authority of the Roman Catholic church in the name of "The Freedom of the Christian Man." However, when Luther, in his turn, saw how the Anabaptists gave new form to Christian freedom in their gathered communities, he turned on them with such fury and violence that religious dissent was eliminated from Germany for hundreds of years. And even the Anabaptists, though they espoused a communism of love, did not hesitate to shun and excommunicate brothers who were found wanting. Jesus was certainly right when he said, "I have not come to bring peace, but a sword" (Matthew 10:34).

The fact is, Christian love has sharp edges, and it has sharp edges because, as Søren Kierkegaard says, "God is always the third party" in every relationship.[20] The very transcendent presence that makes life with others possible through promise and forgiveness is also the presence that discloses the limitedness of that relationship. There is no getting around the fact that ordinary human affections are subordinated to the God-relation. What we cannot expect of Christian love, therefore, is that we can enjoy another person in terms of our own self-satisfaction. Regardless of how naturally good or ideal the bond with another might be, from the Christian point of view love is something held in trust, something given, something I can enjoy only if I do not attempt to possess it.

FURTHER READING

The primary source for the idea of Christian love is the Bible. Most translations would serve the purpose, although the reader should compare several to find one that is most readable. For its introductions, cross references , and other study helps I recommend the *The New Oxford Annotated Bible, Revised Standard Version*, ed. Herbert G. May and Bruce M. Metzger (New York: Oxford University Press, 1973).

Where to begin? Any suggestions are a bit arbitrary, but I would recommend in the Old Testament the books of Genesis and Exodus to establish the narrative of the origins of Israel, Samuel 1 and 2 for the great saga of Saul and David, the Psalms for some of the greatest religious poetry ever written, the book of Isaiah for prophetic expression of Israel's hope, and Hosea for a most remarkable example of forgiving love.

In the New Testament the gospel of Luke and the Book of Acts tell the story of Jesus and the beginnings of the Christian church. The gospels of Matthew and John are also accounts of the life of Jesus and they include specific teachings on the subject of love. The Sermon on the Mount, for example, is found in chapters 5, 6, and 7 of Matthew. The apostle Paul's first letter to the Corinthians contains in chapter 13 the well-known passage beginning, "If I speak in the tongues of men and of angels, but have not love..." Another important statement about the way Christians love can be found in Paul's letter to the Romans, chapter 12. The brief first letter of John (not to be confused with the gospel of John) declares that "God is love."

Anders Nygren's *Agape and Eros*, trans. Philip S. Watson (Philadelphia: Westminster Press, 1953), makes a systematic theological argument that Christian love is only identified with *agape* (divine love) in contrast to *eros* (self-love).

The Mind and Heart of Love, by Martin D'Arcy (New York: Henry Holt & Co., 1947), argues that *agape* and *eros* are not contrary to one another but harmonious.

The Four Loves, by C. S. Lewis (New York: Harvest Book, Harcourt Brace Javanovich, 1960), makes the case from a Christian perspective for four basic kinds of love — affection, friendship, erotic love, and the love of God.

NOTES

1. I Corinthians 15:26. All references and quotations from the Bible are from the Revised Standard Version of the Old and New Testaments, copyrighted in 1952 and 1942.

2. Paul Tillich, *Love, Power, and Justice* (New York: Oxford University Press, 1954), pp. 116–119. See also his *Systematic Theology*, vol. 1 (Chicago: University of Chicago Press, 1951), pp. 279f.

3. Søren Kierkegaard, *Works of Love*, trans. Howard Hong and Edna Hong (London: Collins, 1962), pp. 112f.

4. Karl Barth, *Against the Stream* (London: SCM Press), p. 70. See also pp. 238f.

5. Iris Murdoch, *Metaphysics as a Guide to Morals* (New York: Allen Lane/Penguin Press, 1992), p. 347.

6. Hannah Arendt, *The Human Condition* (Chicago: University of Chicago Press, 1958), p. 238.

7. Ibid., p. 237.

8. Ibid., p. 241.

9. Jaroslav Pelikan, *The Christian Tradition*, vol. 1 (Chicago: University of Chicago Press, 1971), pp. 155, 206.

10. *The Confessions of St. Augustine*, trans. F. J. Sheed (New York: Sheed & Ward, 1943), bk. 8.vii, p. 170.

11. Commenting on the opposition of the desires of the flesh to the Spirit (Galatians 5:17), Augustine says "because the will has sinned, the hard necessity of having sin has pursued the sinner" and that "man's nature was overcome by the fault into which it fell, and so came to lack freedom." *On Man's Perfection in Righteousness*, IV(9), Philip Schaff, ed., *A Select Library of the Nicene and Post-Nicene Fathers of the Christian Church* (New York: Christian Literature Company, 1887), vol. 5, pp. 161–162. See also Augustine's *Confessions*, bk. 8.v, 8.x, and *City of God*, bks. 13 and 14.

12. Two great Protestant theologians, Anders Nygren and Karl Barth, follow Augustine in his emphasis on original sin in order to show the failure of human love. Their arguments make a radical distinction between "eros," self-serving desire that leads to sin and pride, and "agape," the love of God that seeks only the good of the other. Their point seems to be to characterize any form of human love as sinful in contrast to God's absolute sovereignty, on which human salvation depends.

Several comments are in order. Obviously, my distinction between erotic love and Christian love owes much to Nygren. While I certainly agree that Christian love follows from the affirmation of God's transcendence, I would argue that the point of the Christian affirmation is not to discredit human nature, but to re-establish the image of God in man as Paul states in Colossians 3:10. I can agree that there is a difference between erotic love and Christian love without necessarily accepting Nygren's and Barth's judgmental conclusions about the merit of these two kinds of love. Each has its appeal and each has its qualifications, and the qualifications are rather severe.

See Anders Nygren, *Agape and Eros,* trans. Philip S. Watson (Philadelphia: Westminster Press, 1953), pp. 75–80; and Karl Barth, *Church Dogmatics: A Selection,* trans. G. W. Bromiley (New York: 1962), pp. 173–176.
For a Roman Catholic rejoinder, see Martin D'Arcy, *The Mind and Heart of Love* (New York: Holt, Rinehart and Winston, 1947).

13. The reason this negative attitude became the establishment view, Elaine Pagels argues, is that Augustine saw his need to rule his rebellious passions as essentially the same problem as society's need to be ruled by government. Personal purity was analogous to political order. At a time when the Christian church was becoming the religion of empire and no longer a persecuted sect, man's fallen nature made government a necessity. *Adam, Eve, and the Serpent* (New York: Random House, 1988), chap. 5, esp. pp. 105–113.

14. Verna Harrison, *Grace and Human Freedom According to St. Gregory of Nyssa* (Lewiston: Edwin Mellen Press, 1992), p. 142.

15. Quoted by Harrison, pp. 140–141.

16. Quoted by Harrison, p. 136.

17. Blaise Pascal writes: "L'homme n'est ni ange ou bête et le malheur veut que qui veut faire l'ange fait la bête." *Pensées sur la religion et sur Quelques autres sujets,* ed. Louis Lafuma (Paris, 1952), frag. 678, p. 391, par. 1.

18. Elaine Pagels writes: "As we have seen, the majority of Christian converts of the first four centuries regarded the proclamation of moral freedom, grounded in Genesis 1–3, as effectively synonymous with 'the gospel.'" *Adam, Eve and the Serpent,* p. 73, see also p. 76.

19. Tillich, op. cit., p. 68. See also p. 122: "Justice, power, and love towards oneself is rooted in the justice, power, and love which we receive from that which transcends us and affirms us. The relation to ourselves is a function of our relation to God."

20. Kierkegaard, *Works of Love,* p. 124.

Chapter 4

80

ROMANTIC LOVE: TRISTAN AND ISEULT AND HELOISE AND ABELARD

The place of love
Lies not in beaten ways
Nor about our human dwellings.
Love haunts the deserts.

— Gottfried of Strasbourg

To say that romantic love was invented in medieval Western Europe might be claiming too much, since there were parallel developments in Japanese and Persian literature. But there is no doubt that the shape and dynamism peculiar to romantic love in the West has its origins in medieval Christianity and in the chivalric code of the feudal social order.[1] It has, moreover, developed a compelling logic all its own that has carried it beyond its limited aristocratic origin to become almost universally popular in the Western world. Indeed, romantic love is such a powerful idea that for many people this is the first and only real meaning that the word "love" has for them.

The word "romance," of course, is derived from "Roman," having to do with ancient Rome. In the Middle Ages people looked back upon the Roman Empire as something grand and glorious, something far surpassing their own coarse time in its achievements. Eventually the term "romantic" came to refer to almost anything grand and glorious — particularly nature, the forces of nature, and the force of human emotions — in contrast to the ordinary

constraints of daily life and reason and morality. A romantic view
is one that exalts heroic figures and adventurous undertakings—
passionate life as opposed to prudent life.

Romantic love, therefore, refers to those kinds of relationships
in which feeling and high emotion are uppermost. In fact, "a certain
kind of feeling" is regarded as the hallmark of romantic love and
its presence or absence is decisive. It cannot be forced or be made
to happen. Why it comes or goes seems to be unexplainable. It
has a supernatural quality about it: we "fall" in love and are
helpless when it happens. When we are in thrall to love almost
any kind of behavior, no matter how bizarre, seems justifiable.

Life in the Middle Ages was organized almost entirely for war,
and the life of the warrior class centered around the courts of the
barons and lords who were the landowners of the time. A lord's
court principally included his wife and his vassals, warriors who
were beholden to the lord for the lands on which they lived and
maintained their households. These vassals may themselves have
had vassals, other fighting men who depended on them for a
livelihood. The principal occupation of these men was warfare
and tournaments in which they practiced fighting and hunting.
Their main object in life was to protect and extend their domains,
either through fighting or by making alliances through marriage.
Personal feelings played virtually no role in arranging a marriage;
it was essentially a political and economic contract.

To maintain the loyalty of his vassals was of great importance
to every lord, and one of the ways he did this was to keep them in
attendance at his court as much as possible. Thus, he could have
their counsel and support and be relatively sure that they were
not up to mischief on their own or entering into alliances with
some other lord. This meant that they had to learn "courtesy"—
how to live at court with the lord and his lady, who shared in his
power and status. A whole code of conduct, chivalry, developed
to spell out the appropriate forms of behavior for men who fought
on horseback.[2] ("Cheval" is the French word for horse.)

The practice of chivalry, therefore, applied to the men and
women who were members of the aristocracy, the warrior class,
but not to those outside this class. A lady was owed deference
and respect not merely because she was a woman but because of
her lordly status, and this also made her the focus of a great deal
of masculine attention and admiration. To "court" a lady meant

to subordinate oneself to her in order to win her favor and attention. Courtly manners therefore required rough-tempered fighting men to learn politeness and the arts of conversation and music and dance so as to please a lady. Even though the lady may have been hopelessly out of reach because she was the wife of a lord, the idea nevertheless grew that a knight could make himself more noble by submitting himself to a lady.[3] By dedicating his combat to her honor he became more courageous, and by entertaining her with poetry and song he became more genteel, a "gentleman." If at length she responded with a smile or with some more generous gesture, then he would know that he had won her heart because it was done voluntarily; it was outside the duties and constraints of marriage.

This is a crucial element in courtly love—the freedom of both parties. There can be no compulsion in love. The loyalty and devotion that the suitor offers to his lady are given freely, and her response, if she chooses to make one, is a free gift. There is no economic or political necessity that motivates their acts, and there is certainly no moral necessity. The very thing that certifies that it is in fact genuine love is that it is absolutely free.

In several interesting ways the Christian church contributed to the idea of courtly love, albeit unintentionally. First, against the inclination of the landowning barons to arrange marriages as a means of estate management, the church insisted that marriage had to be voluntary. This had the ironic effect of making courtly love affairs appear to be more "moral" (because they were indeed voluntary) than most of the contracted marriages of the time.

Moreover, the church taught that "God is love," and while the priests and bishops may have meant something quite different by this, it had the effect of giving divine sanction to powerful feelings of desire. How could God not be on the side of lovers?

It seems fairly obvious that this notion of love would not have made much sense to the peasants of the Middle Ages, nor would it have seemed very appropriate to the merchants and tradesmen of reviving town life, except to the extent that they imitated courtly society. So this is an idea that appealed mainly to those who understood themselves in terms of the lord-vassal relationship—the warrior aristocracy—and among them it was widely celebrated in poetry and songs and stories. Perhaps the best known of all these stories is the romance of Tristan and Iseult, a story that was told in courtly circles all over Western Europe in one form or

another.[4] "The legend of Isolde" says Henry Adams, "seems to
have served as a sacred book to the women of the twelfth and
thirteenth centuries."[5] The popularity of this poignant portrayal
of love and death soon spread to virtually every social level, and it
became the archetypal image of romantic love which it remains to
this day.

The story tells of Tristan, a vassal of his uncle, King Mark, and
his love for Iseult, Mark's wife. When Tristan first wins the heart
of Iseult, it is in service to his lord; thus his love for her and his
treason to the king are joined in the same act. Their dangerous
love affair consists of one harrowing escapade after another as the
lovers resourcefully deceive the king and outwit their enemies to
pursue their love for one another. Their love has no peace. In fact,
their tormented longing for each other becomes the principal
characteristic of their relationship.[6] Even when they finally manage
to be together in the isolated woods of Morois, they give up their
relative safety to return to their former roles — she as queen and he
as knight — and the flame of their passion is rekindled with even
greater force. At length, after many more vicissitudes and a long
separation (including Tristan's chaste marriage to another woman,
also named Iseult), they are united only in death.

Another medieval love story that seemed to thrive on obstacles
was that of Abelard and Heloise. In contrast to the mythical
romance of Tristan and Iseult, however, this affair actually
happened and the locus was the church, not courtly society.
Abelard was a brilliant and attractive young philosopher in Paris
who quickly achieved fame and popularity as a teacher and skilled
debater. He was retained by the canon of Notre Dame to tutor his
young niece, Heloise, who was also very bright and literate.[7]
Predictably, the two young people fell in love and their affair became
an open scandal. The poet-professor's love songs to Heloise were
sung all over the Latin Quarter. "In popular notions," observes
Henry Adams, "Heloise was Isolde, and would in a moment have
done what Isolde did."[8] Everyone knew about it — except, of
course, Heloise's uncle. When Heloise became pregnant Abelard
offered to marry her to placate her uncle, but Heloise refused to
have him give up his independence. At length, she yielded,
however, and they were married.[9] So as not to compromise
Abelard's career in the church, they struggled unsuccessfully to
keep the marriage a secret. Finally, at Abelard's request, Heloise

"took the veil" and became a nun, and the child was taken by
Abelard's sister. Thinking that Abelard had found a way to
abrogate the marriage, Heloise's uncle was furious at Abelard's
treachery and hired thugs to assault and to castrate him.

Following this catastrophe, Abelard went into monastic
seclusion and later established a convent where Heloise became
the highly respected abbess. The two remained mostly out of touch
for ten years. Communication was restored when Heloise
happened upon a letter written by Abelard to a friend in which he
recited the history of his calamities. When she then wrote to him
she revealed, astonishingly, that her love for Abelard had
diminished not at all and she upbraided him for his inconstancy.
All their travail, long separation, and monastic vows had served
only to heighten the intensity of her feeling for him — and this was
true despite the fact that she knew he was incapable of sexual
response.

THE DEFINING RELATION

As we see, romantic love is impossible love. The totality of
commitment between the lovers is so great that they simply ignore
the impracticality, irrationality, and immorality of their relationship.
There is something literally "otherworldly" about it. So
overwhelming are the odds against it that this kind of love could
only happen if God were somehow present in it, and this is exactly
what Iseult's handmaiden says to her after the lovers have just
narrowly escaped being caught: "God has worked a miracle for
you, Iseult, for he is compassionate and will not hurt the innocent
in heart" (Bédier 50). Even though the lovers betray the most sacred
vows of loyalty — Tristan to his lord and Iseult to her husband —
the innocent totality of their love lifts them above ordinary moral
constraints: "For men see this and that outward thing, but God
alone the heart, and in the heart alone is crime and the sole judge
is God" (Bédier 56). Quite consistently, neither Tristan nor Iseult
will concede the slightest bit of guilt when they are called upon to
repent: "I will not say one word of penance for my love," says
Iseult adamantly (Bédier 68f, 80).

With similar reasoning, Heloise is equally stubborn in her
unrepentance, having learned from Abelard the theological
distinction that intention alone is blameworthy, not the act or its

consequences. And it is not to God that she pleads, but to Abelard: "If I am hurting you exceedingly, I am, as you know, exceedingly innocent."[10]

How can this be? — especially in a Christian society that places the highest value on faith in God and in the sacred bonds between vassal and lord and between wife and husband? The answer is that romantic love could only happen in just such a society where an absolute and unqualified commitment is called for, but where a commitment that should apply only to God is directed instead to one's beloved. Reading Heloise's letters to Abelard, notes Étienne Gilson, "one is struck immediately by the omnipresence of Abelard and the total absence of God." And God is not merely absent from her letters, continues Gilson, "He is continually being expelled from them."[11] The displacement is obvious and deliberate. From a Christian point of view, in other words, romantic love is a kind of idolatry, a perversion of Christian love. There is, to be sure, a certain purity of heart in its utter selflessness but it is offered up to a fallible human being in the place of God.

Heloise's relation to Abelard clearly reveals this essential selflessness, but because it is an assertion of her freedom, not mere submissiveness, the male-female roles are reversed and she claims a kind of parity with him. She has subordinated her freedom to him but at the same time the consciousness of her act as a free gift has made her strong in her self. The resulting ambivalence is apparent in the opening salutation of her first letter to him: "To her lord, or rather, father; to her husband, or rather, brother; from his servant, or rather daughter; his wife, or rather sister: To Abelard from Heloise."[12] There is certainly no courtly deference in what follows. She bitterly complains of his neglect and boldly lays claim to his love "because of the love I have always borne you, as everyone knows, a love which is beyond all bounds." Her audacious language makes the totality of her devotion unmistakably clear: "You know, beloved, as the whole world knows, how much I have lost in you...You are the sole cause of my sorrow, and you alone can grant me the grace of consolation. You alone have the power to make me sad, to bring me happiness or comfort."[13]

The depth of her passion does not blind Heloise to what she is doing. She knows full well that her love for Abelard is idolatrous: "At every stage of my life up to now," she says to him, "I have feared to offend you rather than God, and tried to please you more than him" (*Letters* 134). Indeed, there is good reason to believe that Heloise's love for Abelard is quite deliberately modeled on what she learned from him about the love of God. Abelard was, after all, one of the best philosophers of his day and he was her teacher. As Irving Singer suggests, Heloise's love "patterns itself after the dogmas of the man she reveres. Seeking to get him to reciprocate, what better way than to assert that she has always loved him as he himself said everyone should love God. In other words: you are a god to me, and will you not therefore be merciful?"[14]

The outspoken honesty of Heloise's letters to Abelard reveals more sharply the Christian dimension implicit in this kind of love — the ascription of transcendent value to one's beloved. This is the defining relation. Her frank acknowledgment that she has substituted Abelard for God is only a little more extreme than the courtly lover's pledge of absolute devotion to his lordly lady. Every obstacle, every limitation, serves not to bring the lover down to earth but only increases the devotion necessary to surmount the difficulty. No test is great enough to exhaust the lover's freedom to give of himself. The achievement of love's goal becomes not nearly as important as the dedication, the singleness of purpose, necessary to sustain the relationship. This yearning, this passion, is how the lover knows that this is "true love" and the intensity of this feeling is its primary credential. Like erotic love, romantic love thrives on what it does not have. As with erotic love, success could be the worst thing that could happen. Passion, not happiness, is its aim.

THE ROLE OF REASON

Undeniably there is an erotic aspect to romantic love. The tension and suffering of the lovers' longing is what makes it so poignant. Music especially seems to have the power to convey these feelings and nowhere is this painful yearning expressed more beautifully than in Richard Wagner's operatic version of Tristan and Iseult, especially the *Liebestod* theme in the third act, which ascends to an almost unearthly level of intensity. Few human experiences can match this kind of feeling in its power to concentrate the mind and the emotions. No wonder that the ecstatic

moments of romantic love are so dislocating to ordinary life and so
unforgettable forever afterward.

But there is a fundamental difference between erotic love and
romantic love. In erotic love, as we have seen, the disproportion
between the infinite devotion of the lover (what he wants) and the
finite actuality of the beloved (what he gets) leads the lover to see
the limitations of the object of his desire and to move on to
something more promising. He is, after all, pursuing the good—
what is to his ultimate self-interest. But romantic love in its purest
essence is selfless. Having been tutored by Christianity it lacks the
calculating, self-regarding element that is characteristic of erotic
love. Indeed, the otherworldliness of romantic love is so strong
that self-annihilation actually may be an inducement—the only
prospect powerful enough to prove the totality of the lover's
devotion. For example, when Tristan calls to Iseult one night, after
they have returned from their woodland retreat, she knows full
well what they are risking: "Ah, what do you ask? That I come?
No. Remember Ogrin the hermit, and the oaths sworn by me. Be
still, death waits for us...What does death matter? You call me,
you want me, I come!" (Bédier 98).

Heloise is equally reckless in the abandon with which she has
given herself to Abelard. "I was powerless to oppose you in
anything," she says to him, "I found strength at your command to
destroy myself" (*Letters* 113). Even entering the convent, she notes,
was not done out of piety but only because he asked her to do so:
"God knows, I would not have hesitated to follow you or to precede
you into hell itself (*ad Vulcania loca*) if you had given the order. My
heart was not my own, but yours. Even now, more than ever
before, if it is not with you it is nowhere, for you are its very
existence."[15]

As we saw in Plato, erotic love is essentially rational in its desire
for quality and discriminating continuity. The integrity of the self
and its world is fostered by the pursuit of the good, the true, and
the beautiful. While an inflammatory madness may instigate desire,
as described by Plato in the *Phaedrus* (244), it is ultimately brought
to heel by the more basic need for coherence and unity. But what
is the erotic function in romantic love? Here, too, it seeks unity but
this is achieved by emotional intensity rather than logical
connectedness. Perversely, it seems, the self-interest of romantic
love is found only in total "otherness," in the moments of absolute

self-giving when the lover, like a trapeze artist, abandons himself into thin air with only the hope that he will be caught by his beloved. This self-sacrificial impulse, prompted by the radical freedom of Christian love, is what makes romantic love so daring and breathtakingly exciting. By comparison to this, the "folly" of which the apostle Paul speaks (I Corinthians 1:21) seems like a tame somersault over a safety net.

THE ROLE OF SEXUALITY

In no other concept of love does sexuality receive as strong an endorsement as in romantic love. In the Middle Ages this was largely a reaction against the attitude that the function of sex in marriage was for the production of children in order to perpetuate and extend the domains of the nobility. Love had little to do with it. According to W.T.H. Jackson, this was the question that the troubadours and poets of love sought to resolve: "How can love be reconciled with a social order which recognizes sex only in marriage but regards marriage as a contract made without love?"[16] The answer was to switch the importance of sex from its reproductive function (in marriage) to its expressive power (outside of marriage). In neither the story of Tristan and Iseult nor Heloise's letters is there even the slightest mention of the reproductive consequences of sexual love. The generation of children is the concern of marriage, not romantic love.

The focus on intensity of feeling coincides nicely with the intoxication of the senses experienced in sexual excitement. The confusion of the latter with the former is probably humankind's easiest mistake to make and, indeed, how could one in fact form a clear distinction? The high-minded denigrate the latter as "lust," while the former is praised as "true love." But when one is in it, do they not look and feel the same? Is it not possible, moreover, that the two stand in some causal relation to each other? If self-surrender is the crux of romantic love, then what is more likely to overwhelm prudential concerns of self-regard than powerful sexual feelings? And, conversely, what is more likely to release one's powers of feeling and sensation than the gift of one's freedom to another?

The intense sexuality of romantic love is probably also accentuated by its focus on the individuality of the lovers. The body of the beloved is uniquely important because it is the *means* by which her or his freedom is given to the lover, but it is at the same time that which *limits* the expression of that love. It separates as well as unites. The ingenuity of romantic lovers is thus endlessly tested to find new ways of overcoming their physical separation at the same time that their separateness is enhanced. Each summons the other to the fullest embodiment of freedom in a kind of "mutual enchantment" (to use the language of Jean-Paul Sartre), which is both powerful and ambiguous – as we shall see in chapter 6.

While it is true that not all courtly love affairs were consummated, the sexual undercurrent is unmistakably present. The lady's sexual favors may have been long deferred, but they are the tangible signs of her love that were sought by her lover. In the story of Tristan and Iseult the sexual nature of their passion is made plainly evident from the outset, although its significance is sometimes discounted as due to the magical potion they drink. The potion, concocted by Iseult's mother, was intended for Iseult and King Mark on their wedding night, but was inadvertently drunk by Tristan and Iseult instead. But the potion was not so much cause as effect. Iseult had already observed Tristan (in his bath!) and "saw that he was beautiful" (Bédier 25). (Iseult's desire is even more evident in Gottfried von Strassburg's version.[17]) And when Tristan "won" Iseult, supposedly for King Mark, he had already proven his devotion and his willingness to give his life to her. The wine they drink together is "magical" because it is the moment when they recognize what is happening to them. Something supernatural has entered their lives. "I knew I loved you," lovers sometimes say, "when I saw how you brushed the hair from your eyes." Drinking the wine is sacramental, if you will: It is the outward and visible occasion when their love is made manifest.

The two are then made wretched by their desire for one another until one evening, as the story says, "they gave themselves up utterly to love" (Bédier 35). From then on they are insatiable: "Love pressed them hard, as thirst presses the dying stag to the stream" and everyone could see "their every sense overflowing like new wine working in the vat" (Bédier 42-43).

It is not until later in the story, however, that we begin to see that their love is not simply a sexual relationship. When they are

alone together in the woods of Morois, the king happens upon
them while they are sleeping (with their clothes on, fortunately)
and sees Tristan's naked sword between them. He concludes,
naively, that their relationship is a chaste one and this sets the
stage for their rehabilitation and return to their former roles as
queen and knight. True, the sword is a symbol of chastity, but its
appearance in the story seems almost accidental. Moreover, it
strains credulity to think that a pair of lovers would sleep with a
drawn sword between them. What does the sword mean?

Remember that Tristan loves Iseult as a lady, a queen, and he
is her vassal. But in the woods together she is not a queen and he
is not a vassal. Their love languishes. Tristan laments that Iseult
was a queen at King Mark's side, "but in this wood she lives a
slave, and I waste her youth"(Bédier 78). In other words, their
love, while it is otherworldly in its aspirations, requires the
separations of worldly roles for its intensity. There has to be a
sword between them in order for them to be in love. In a perverse
sort of way, romantic lovers actually need the world in order to
continually transcend it and thereby keep their "heavenly love"
alive. Overcoming obstacles of practicality and morality is what
makes their love other-than-worldly. This also helps to keep desire
intensely focused on the beloved, since the erotic can never be
satisfied enough to move on. What the two want is not each other
so much as the great longing that each feels for the other. Quite
predictably when Iseult returns to King Mark's court and is restored
to honor, the passion of the two lovers rises to new levels of mad
intensity.

In the era of courtly love, this element of tension and conflict
with worldly values was considered so essential that it was virtually
a requirement that true love be adulterous love. The famous
judgment of the countess of Champagne was that love could not,
in principle, exist between husband and wife: "For indeed lovers
grant one another all things mutually and freely, without being
impelled by any motive of necessity, whereas husband and wife
are held by their duty to submit their wills to each other and to
refuse each other nothing."[18]

It is, however, in Heloise's passion for Abelard that we find the
brightest light cast on this crucial issue. There is no doubt that
their love was preeminently sexual in its inception. Heloise recalls
quite candidly the pleasures of the flesh that she enjoyed with

Abelard when she was the envy of women everywhere because of his brilliant reputation and the love songs and verses that he wrote in her praise (*Letters* 115). What is more, the memories of the sweet pleasures they shared are still very much alive with her. "I am still young and full of life," she writes, "I love you more than ever and suffer bitterly from living a life for which I have no vocation." Her longing for him makes a fraud of her reputation for piety and spiritual discipline as abbess of her convent. At every turn she is tormented by these memories — even when the Mass is being celebrated:

> When prayer should be purest, the obscene imagining of these pleasures so completely overwhelms my poor soul that I yield to their shameful delectation rather than to prayer. I who should tremble at what I have done, sigh over what I have lost. Nor is it only what we have done but the very places, the moments which we have been together that are so deeply graven into my heart that once more I see them with you in all their plenitude. I cannot escape from them even in my sleep. Sometimes the very movements of my body show forth the thoughts of my soul, betraying themselves in involuntary words.[19]

That she continues to stoke these fires of sensual passion seems particularly amazing in light of Abelard's emasculation.

But that is not the real issue, she insists. His neglect and indifference are proof to her that his love never was anything more than lust. As much as she burns with memories of sexual pleasure, she knows that what she really wants transcends sexual love. Even though Abelard is incapable of sexual response, Heloise does not give up. If his love had been genuine, she angrily charges, it would have overcome all that happened to them and he would care for her still. She cites her own undying love for him as proof of what she means: "I have finally denied myself every pleasure in obedience to your will, kept nothing for myself . . . I am yours" (*Letters* 117). So, again, as with Tristan and Iseult, even though sexual feeling is most strongly affirmed, what counts ultimately in romantic love reaches beyond sexuality.

The contrast with erotic love is again apparent: Erotic love is always seeking something *better*, whereas in romantic love the beloved is *God* — as Abelard is to Heloise. What could be better? The fact that they are husband and wife, technically still married, she brushes aside as totally irrelevant: "God knows I never sought anything in you except yourself; I wanted simply you, nothing of yours. I looked for no marriage bond, no marriage portion." In even more acerbic language, she denounces the security of marriage: "The name of wife may seem more sacred or more binding, but sweeter for me will always be the word mistress, or, if you will permit me, that of concubine or whore" (*Letters* 113).

Here Heloise puts her finger on the crucial factor in romantic love—freedom. She would rather be Abelard's whore because then she could be sure he wanted her for herself alone and not out of some sense of obligation. To Heloise, marriage means something very public and worldly—"a contract of convenience" that carried many social and legal consequences—quite contrary, says C.N.L. Brooke, to her idea of "a love which was wholly unselfish, which consisted entirely in giving—without any thought of or corruption by reward."[20] She had tried to dissuade him from marriage, she reminds him, "But you kept silent about most of my arguments for preferring love to wedlock and freedom to chains" (*Letters* 114). Note how she pairs love with freedom. As desperately as she wants him, Heloise knows that any formal security, like marriage, will in fact not guarantee their love but will actually preclude what she wants—the free gift of himself to her. Heloise is a shining heroine of romantic love because she is so fiercely aware of what she wants and will settle for nothing less. Nothing else will do because only this is love.

The key consideration, therefore, is not that romantic love must be adulterous, as the courtly lovers implied, but that it be free.[21] What is most highly prized in romantic love is passionate feeling, and this is most intense when all bounds and constraints are overleaped. It is as contrary to morality and marriage as anything could possibly be. Its origin in the Middle Ages was a clear affirmation that love is more important than the sanctity of marriage. The ironic thing is that in modern times the notion of romantic love has become established, not as the antithesis of marriage, but as its necessary precondition. The question remains whether the otherworldly yearning of romantic love is any more adaptable to the modern economic and social functions of marriage than it was in the Middle Ages. The fact that most modern stories of romantic love *end* with marriage would suggest that the fundamental logic of romantic love has not changed.

OUTCOMES

To be fair to Abelard we should note that he does not dispute Heloise's accusations. "My love," he concedes, "which brought us both to sin, should be called lust, not love. I took my fill of my wretched pleasures in you, and this was the sum total of my love" (*Letters* 153). He even admits that leading her into the convent might have been a way of keeping her for himself when he withdrew from the world (*Letters* 149). Somewhat lamely, he excuses his neglect of her in the convent because he did not think she needed his assistance; he was confident of her abilities to carry out her duties as abbess (*Letters* 119).

But all these misdirected motives have turned out for the best, argues Abelard, because through their suffering God has acted mercifully, setting him "wholly free from the heavy yoke of carnal desire" (*Letters* 148), and enabling Heloise to "turn the curse of Eve into the blessing of Mary" (*Letters* 150). What has befallen them is not God's punishment but God's mercy, designed to convert them from worldly desires to a true relationship to God. He urges her, therefore, to accept her new role as a "bride of Christ" and to become "his sister in Christ" (*Letters* 119, 137).

Abelard still has one thing to ask of her, however. He is in fear of imminent death, and he wants Heloise to assure him that his body will be brought to her convent so that it will be buried in consecrated ground. Heloise prays that she will not live to see that day because his death would extinguish the meaning of her life (*Letters* 128). The difference between them is here made quite clear: Abelard sees that the course of their love, despite its selfish sensuality, is leading them back to its true origin, to God. Heloise, on the contrary, can only see Abelard's death as her death. "If I lose you," she asks, "what is left for me to hope for?" (*Letters* 129).

As it happened, Abelard did precede Heloise in death (by twenty-one years), and she did have his body moved to her convent burying ground where she was eventually buried beside him. Still later their bones were moved again and they now lie together, very romantically, in a gothic tomb in the Pere Lachaise Cemetery in Paris.

The mythical romance of Tristan and Iseult also ends in death and parallels what happens to Abelard and Heloise in a few interesting ways. Long separated from Iseult, Tristan dies from wounds suffered in battle before Iseult can reach him, despite her belief that they are fated to die together. She then dies of grief beside his body. King Mark has them buried in separate tombs but a green and leafy briar springs from Tristan's tomb and falls to root at Iseult's tomb. Like Abelard and Heloise, it is only in death that the lovers are finally united.

If romantic love is indeed a passion that surpasses all worldly bounds, then it is not surprising that death, as a release from the world, is its logical outcome. Denis de Rougemont argues that the dark secret of romantic love is that it is really in love with death rather than life.[22] But if this is so, why is it the almost universal testimony of lovers that they "never felt so much alive" as when they were in love? The answer, I think, is that this is when they are most keenly aware of the full reach of their freedom. They do not so much want death as defy it. Death, too, can be surpassed.

ASSESSMENT

What can we expect of romantic love?

At the very least romantic love carries with it a sense of grandeur. Elegance of manner and atmosphere, politeness, rules of etiquette — all derive from respect due to a noble lady and from the mutual respect that autonomous lovers owe each other. At the heart of the courtly tradition is the fundamental recognition that love is the free gift of the other. If a man wants to win the affections of one who is sovereign, the first necessity is to show due regard for her sovereignty. The rules provide a certain form in language and manner for both lover and beloved to follow, and the willful submission to these rules generates some of the intensity that makes romantic love so enticing. Feeling, after all, is what romantic love is all about, and the voluntary constraint of freedom within certain forms and procedures enhances the meaning and expression of feeling. But of course everyone knows that the presence of the form does not mean that the feeling is necessarily present within. This uncertain possibility is itself interesting and exciting, and, for the romantic, may be more important than the truth.

The prospect of this delightful uncertainty forces the romantic lover to focus very precisely on the other. Sensitivity to the subtlest nuances of mood and behavior are critically important so that no hint of feeling is missed. The possibility that love may be freely given or withheld means that the individuality of the beloved must be treated with great attentiveness.

What makes romantic love not only grand but also glorious, however, is its willingness—nay, its necessity—to breach every limit and constraint in its devotion to the other. To everyone but the lover this appears as absolute madness, but to the lover the utter irrationality of this feeling is self-validating. It needs no other justification; it has no other support.

There is something undeniably admirable about the selfless, heroic quality of romantic love, and it endures as a poetic ideal of what love ought to be, even though its impracticality, irrationality, or immorality are usually deplored in actual life. But romantic love virtually guarantees suffering—partly because the romantic lover wants this kind of intensity; he must have the pain of separation and longing that he feels as love—and partly because the object of his devotion cannot possibly measure up to the totality of the lover's devotion. Disappointment, disillusionment, and despair are inevitable—but even that bitterness may be cherished by the lover because it is the residue of the inward compaction of self that love brought to him.

FURTHER READING

One of the primary sources for this discussion of romantic love is *The Romance of Tristan and Iseult*, retold by Joseph Bédier, trans. Hilaire Belloc, and completed by Paul Rosenfeld (New York: Vintage Books, Random House, 1945). Another version of the story can be found in A. T. Hatto's *Gottfried von Strassburg, "Tristan," With the Surviving Fragments of the Tristan of Thomas, Newly Translated. With an Introduction* (Harmondsworth: Penguin, 1960).

The other main source for this discussion is *The Letters of Abelard and Heloise*, trans. with an Introduction by Betty Radice (Harmondsworth: Penguin, 1974). The Introduction is very helpful in establishing the historical context and the Select Bibliography has additional suggestions for background reading.

Almost as important as the primary sources in this case is Denis de Rougemont's *Love in the Western World* (New York: Pantheon Books, 1956) because of its controversial focus on the Tristan myth as the archetypal model of passion in conflict with marriage.

Other helpful studies used in this discussion include:

C.N.L. Brooke, *The Medieval Idea of Marriage* (Oxford: Oxford University Press, 1989)

Étienne Gilson, *Heloise and Abelard* (Ann Arbor: University of Michigan Press, 1960)

W.T.H. Jackson, *The Anatomy of Love* (New York: Columbia University Press, 1971)

Irving Singer, *The Nature of Love*, vol. 2 *Courtly and Romantic* (Chicago: University of Chicago Press, 1984)

NOTES

1. "In no other epoch did the ideal of civilization amalgamate to such a degree with that of love. Just as scholasticism represents the grand effort of the medieval spirit to unite all philosophic thought in a single centre, so the theory of courtly love, in a less elevated sphere, tends to embrace all that appertains to the noble life." J. Huizinga: *The Waning of the Middle Ages* (Garden City, N.Y.: Doubleday Anchor, 1954), p. 108.

2. "The priests resident at the princely courts used the resources of scholastic analysis to draw up precise rules for the complex rites which were to govern the respective behavior of the gentlemen and the well-born woman in noble society....Any man who wished to be admitted to courtly gatherings had to conform to them. He was expected to choose a lady and to serve her." Georges Duby: *The Age of the Cathedrals* (Chicago: University of Chicago Press, 1981), p. 254.

3. "A man would be a better knight if he loved—in fact it was doubtful whether a man who did not adore a lady could be a true knight." Sidney Painter: *French Chivalry* (Ithaca: Cornell University Press, 1940), p. 113.

4. Our discussion is based on the retelling by Joseph Bédier, trans. Hilaire Belloc and completed by Paul Rosenfeld, *The Romance of Tristan and Iseult* (New York: Vintage Books, Random House, 1945), which was assembled mainly from versions originating in the twelfth and thirteenth centuries.

5. Henry Adams, *Mont-Saint-Michel and Chartres* (Garden City, N.Y.: Doubleday Anchor Books, 1959), p. 241.

6. Curiously, however, neither the Bédier version nor the one told by Gottfried von Strassburg exactly reflect the courtly venue: "He (Gottfried) rejects totally the idea of love service and the subordination of the man to the woman and substitutes for it a partnership which is based on sexual attraction and recognition in the other of the fulfillment of a need," a need as great for the woman as for the man, says W.T.H. Jackson, *The Anatomy of Love* (New York: Columbia University Press, 1971), p. 64.

7. According to C.N.L. Brooke, the practice of concubines and the children of canons living in cathedral quarters was widespread in the twelfth

century. It is in this context, he suggests, that Heloise became familiar with unconsecrated love relationships that "were widely tolerated and still in some sense respectable." *The Medieval Idea of Marriage* (Oxford: Oxford University Press, 1989), p. 83, See also pp. 90–91, 261–262.

8. Adams, *Mont-Saint-Michel*, p. 240.

9. The marriage, however, was "quite illegal," since Abelard was a canon. Brooke, *Medieval Idea*, p. 106.

10. *Epist. II, PL* 168:186A, quoted and translated by Étienne Gilson, *Heloise and Abelard* (Ann Arbor: University of Michigan Press, 1960), p. 59.

11. Gilson, *Heloise and Abelard*, p. 88.

12. Heloise, *Epist. II, PL* 178:181 B., quoted by Gilson, *Heloise and Abelard*, p. 102.

13. *The Letters of Abelard and Heloise*, trans. with an Introduction by by Betty Radice (New York: Penguin Books, 1974), p. 113.

14. Irving Singer, *The Nature of Love*, vol. 2, *Courtly and Romantic* (Chicago: University of Chicago Press, 1984), p. 96.

15. *Epist. II, PL* 178:186–87, quoted and translated by Gilson, *Heloise and Abelard*, p. 92. Cf. *Letters* 117.

16. Jackson, *Anatomy of Love*, p. 37.

17. "She looked him up and down; and whatever a maid may survey in a man all pleased her very well, and she praised it in her thoughts. And now that her scrutiny had shown his figure to be so magnificent and his manners so princely, her heart spoke within her." A. T. Hatto, *Gottfried von Strassburg, "Tristan," With the Surviving Fragments of the Tristan of Thomas, Newly Translated, With an Introduction.* (Harmondsworth: Penguin, 1960), p. 173.

18. Denis de Rougemont, *Love in the Western World* (New York: Pantheon Books, 1956), p. 34n.

19. *Epist. IV, PL* 178:196–97, quoted and translated by Gilson, *Heloise and Abelard*, pp. 76–77. Cf. *Letters* 133.

20. Brooke, *Medieval Idea*, pp. 261–262.

21. "Most of all, romantic love has to be understood as an emotion that thrives on freedom, as an emotion built around mobility and choice, as a lack of determinacy that we sometimes choose to ignore by pretending that love is primarily a matter of fate." Robert C. Solomon, *Love – Emotion, Myth and Metaphor* (Garden City, N.Y.: Anchor/Doubleday, 1981), p. 141.

22. Rougemont, *Love in the Western World*, pp. 42–46.

Chapter 5

ℰↃ

MORAL LOVE: IMMANUEL KANT AND SØREN KIERKEGAARD

...love is not love
Which alters when it alteration finds,
Or bends with the remover to remove.
O no! it is an ever-fixed mark,
That looks on tempests and is never shaken.
— William Shakespeare

Intensity of feeling may be the sufficient validating credential of love for some, but others insist that mere passion is not enough. There must be something further, they argue, that qualifies love as "true" or "right," as opposed to that which is merely infatuation or lust. The "trueness" of love cannot be found in its intensity, which may wax or wane, but in its moral nature. For many people this moral significance is provided by the family or by institutions, such as the church, or by the state in its legal certification of the relationship. Implicit in all of these is the recognition that human relationships are necessarily subordinate to some larger social-historical context and derive their legitimacy from that context. "No man is an island," says John Donne, and neither do love affairs take place on an island. There are at least two families involved, there is a community with its cultural standards, and there is a state that must uphold laws, guarantee contracts, and so forth. Love is social and carries with it a series of social obligations.

While all this is true enough, and the elders and moralists of every community never fail to warn us about the immaturity of romantic notions that lack the responsibilities that go with love, there is something unsatisfying about defining the "rightness" of love in terms of conformity to criteria external to the relation itself. One of the appealing things about romantic love is that its excitement and intensity provide a self-verifying stamp of authenticity in its very nature. It answers to no other judge. We know that we are in love because of how we feel. The question is, does so-called true love have something similarly intrinsic that guarantees its legitimacy?

For Immanuel Kant, an eighteenth-century German philosopher, this guarantee is to be found in our rational nature. What is distinctive about human nature, Kant argues, is the rational form that we give to our experience. Our innate capacity to see nature in terms of lawful principles—cause and effect, for example—is what makes science possible. In a similar way, the application of rational principle to human actions is what makes moral experience possible. Reason shows us not only the scientific laws that govern nature, but also the moral principles that should govern our behavior. Our sense of what ought to be in any given situation, says Kant, is not determined so much by the past or the present as by our capacity to reason consistently.[1] Desires and inclinations tell us only what we want, but reason has the capacity to tell us what *ought* to be the case independently of these impulses. It is precisely because we have a choice between what our inclinations tell us and what reason tells us that we are moral creatures.[2] We are free to follow our inclinations or to act rationally. In either case we are responsible for our actions.

Reason, Kant argue, tells us two things in our relations with others. It tells us, first of all, that the rational nature of every person must receive the same respect and due regard that we expect for ourselves. "Rational nature exists as an end in itself," says Kant (FPMM 46). In other words, each person is autonomous, an end in himself, and not merely a means for the achievement of another's end. "Rational beings...are called persons," says Kant (FPMM 45). Second, reason tells us that whatever we do in our relation to another person should be based on a principle that can be universalized. That is to say, while we are self-legislating, we must legislate to ourselves as persons of principle, not merely as creatures of impulse and desire.[3] Moreover, the principle of our action cannot be merely self-regarding or self-justifying. It must be capable of extension to everyone else under the same conditions.

Note that these two guidelines do not tell us *what* to do. Nor do they tell us what love is. They only tell us that whatever we do, a relationship must have a certain rational consistency. It is the *form* of the relationship that must be right. Whatever the specifics of the relationship might be, we know beforehand that a morally right relationship ought to show these two characteristics: mutual respect and rational consistency.

In Kant's thinking the intelligible world is governed both by forces that draw humankind together (love) and forces that keep them separate (respect). Moral life is lived in this tension between attraction and repulsion. Mary Gregor observes, "A maxim of love without respect, or of respect without love, would not really be a moral relation at all."[4] Our duties to others always involve both of these considerations, with sometimes one and sometimes the other being more prominent.

Thus the appeal of this view is its dignity. Lover and beloved regard each other as autonomous, each fully respecting the sovereign powers of reason and choice in the other. The pleasure they take in each other is not in the passions, which are selfish in their aim, but in the gratification of their mutual rationality because this is what truly unites them. Neither partner would seek to exploit the other and any kind of domination or submission would be necessarily precluded. The strong sense of moral obligation that each feels for the other arises out of their rational natures and their principled relation to each other, not from external constraints imposed on them by society.

What they wish for each other is nothing less than the fulfillment of rational virtue. How to achieve this in a loving relationship must be left open, since there is so much diversity in cultural practices, models of sexual behavior, and complexities of relationships. Carol Gilligan has shown, for example, that there may be a fundamental difference between the way girls and boys think about moral issues.[5] Problems arise, not because we do not know what to do, but because of conflicting moral claims. But this is why Kantian principles are "empty." They do not tell us specifically what to do because, at bottom, what they call for is openness to reexamination, to reconsideration. The "form" of moral love is not so much a rule of conduct as it is a way of testing all rules. To be moral, in other words, is to be accountable—to be always ready to bring one's actions under rational scrutiny. "In short," Henry Aiken observes, "I am always bound to listen to reason, and this means, in part, that the process of moral reconsideration and justification is never finally closed, even when, for the time being, I find that I must provisionally make up my mind."[6] At its best, moral love would be just this kind of accountability—beginning with one's partner but extending to humankind as a whole.

To be sure, such a high-minded view of love may not often be experienced in real life. Some of Kant's critics have called it an "ethic of the angels." Kant himself thought that the irresolvable conflict between self-love and love of others made such an ideal of love a practical impossibility. "But the Idea is true," he nonetheless insists, because the idea of love as perfect reciprocity is necessary as a standard by which to measure our relations with others.[7] Upholding this moral ideal, even though it is not fully achievable, continues to be important to those who feel that true love must be something more than the uncertainty of impulsive emotions or restless desires.

While Kant's view is admirable in its clear affirmation of the autonomous consciousness as the key to a moral, loving relationship, his cool rationality and legalistic language are a bit off-putting. Keep in mind that the issue here is integrity. Kant achieves this by insisting that love, as well as everything else, should submit to the rule of reason. Another way to achieve integrity is to focus on the will because the power of choice is at the very heart of moral consistency.

This is the approach taken by Søren Kierkegaard in his first main work, *Either/Or*. Through a variety of literary devices he leads the reader to see that choice is the secret of *either* an interesting "aesthetic" life (volume 1) *or* an "ethical" life (volume 2). Discussions of literature, music, and, finally, the tale of the seduction of a young girl make the first volume cleverly entertaining. In the second volume Kierkegaard presents a fictional character, Judge William, who makes an impassioned defense of married love against the purely sensual and aesthetic love articulated by the clever young sophisticate named Johannes in the first volume. To counter the young aesthete's exclusive focus on the enjoyment of the moment, the judge insists that conjugal love is the transfiguration of the moment.[8] His point is that the aesthete's obsession with sensuous intensity is inevitably discontinuous and fragmentary. Johannes pursues love for the moments of excitement it can provide and then breaks it off before it can become dull or boring. The subsequent void leads only to despair and self-alienation. Conjugal love, on the other hand, because it is a reaffirmation of the moment, leads to a continuous history and acquisition of the self.

For the young aesthete any attempt to see the moral dimension of love is absolutely rejected. For him "duty is the enemy of love" (EO 468). Why? Because any constraint of freedom makes impossible the delicious uncertainty that romantic love consists of. To the judge, however, duty is not the constraint of freedom, but is in fact the internalization of freedom. Only by the reaffirmation of one's first love does one acquire continuity, that is, a history, a self. In constantly repossessing one's first love, one is in effect gaining possession of one's self. This is why the judge says, "In marriage...the main thing is what is inward" (EO 472). The aesthete, by contrast, loses himself by his disengagement from the moment when it is no longer interesting. He becomes fragmented into separate instants that he no longer "owns."

We see, therefore, two different ways of solving the problem of "true love" by finding an intrinsic factor. For Kant, a loving relation is made moral by the lovers' conformity of their freedom to universal principles. It is rational principle that provides the constancy which transcends the vagaries of uncertain moments and emotional ups and downs. For Kierkegaard, the morality of conjugal love consists in its history and continuity, the welding together of discrete, disparate moments by the lovers' commitment. The continuous reappropriation of each moment of the loving relationship is what achieves moral substance.

THE DEFINING RELATION

A conventional view of love as moral is to see the loving relationship as subject to an external authority, such as a religious body or the state, which confers legitimacy on the relationship and imposes certain concomitant obligations. The morality of the relationship thus depends on conforming to a standard or set of rules *outside* the relationship itself. One could argue, of course, that by submitting themselves to the rules, the lovers have incorporated them into the relationship. It is not so much a case of love versus the rules, but rather—as in the case of some ethnic traditions—that the rules are what make the relationship possible in the first place. In traditions where marriages are arranged, for example, it is expected that love is the *result* rather than the motive for marriage. Nonetheless, morality in this case still seems derivative of something else and not a function of the loving relationship itself.

A more intrinsic view would be to see the duties of lovers on the model of professional ethics. A doctor's duty, for example, is to care for the physical health of his patients. His duty and his professional identity are virtually indistinguishable: if he does not care for the health of his patients, then he is not a real doctor. Similarly, one could say that a true lover is one who cares for his beloved. If he does not, then he is a false lover. Thus, the nature of the duty is intrinsic to the function being performed. If we properly understand what it means to be a doctor or a lover, then we know what each one's respective duties are.

There are several problems with this. One is that while we have a relatively concrete notion of what a doctor is and what his duties are, it is not so clear what it means to be a lover or what love's duties are. Human love takes so many varied forms that it would seem to be impossible to identify some specific characteristics that pertain to all lovers—anywhere, any time. And how would disputes be adjudicated? By a panel of well-known lovers?

Moreover, we are not comfortable with the notion that love has duties. The possibility that a lover is acting out of a sense of obligation seems antithetical to true love. We may in fact expect that a lover will do certain things, but the presence of compulsion kills their significance. We have learned from Christian love and from romantic love that love must be a free gift.

Finally, the problem of constancy is not solved. What is usually meant by "true love" is that it is forever—or at least that it is enduring. As Judge William says, it should have "the stamp of the eternal" upon it (EO 393). The problem with the doctor analogy is that one could, if necessary, easily quit the duties of a doctor by leaving the medical profession. This is exactly what a true lover may not do.

Nevertheless, even with these difficulties in mind, this example is instructive because it shows the possibility of finding the moral dimension of love through an understanding of its intrinsic nature. As with Kant and Kierkegaard, it is apparent that the crucial factor is the form of the commitment that the lover makes. What defines love as moral is the nature of the relation itself. The character of the beloved must necessarily be of secondary significance. The sense of duty or moral obligation arises because the lover has identified himself with a universal principle (Kant) or with conjugal fidelity (Kierkegaard) or with a professional role (as in the case of the doctor). Certain moral necessities emerge as a consequence of this choice of identity. The duties of love, if you will, are essentially duties to one's self.

The logic of moral love is now made clear. The lover is not so much committed to the beloved as he is committed to the relationship. And he is committed to sustaining the relationship at whatever cost because this is who he is. He cannot give up the relationship because this would be tantamount to surrendering his identity.

For Kierkegaard's Judge William it all comes down to fundamental choice: "Choice itself is decisive for a personality's content; in choice personality immerses itself in what is chosen, and when it does not choose it wastes consumptively away" (EO 482). "What is chosen" does not refer so much to the beloved as to a certain way of life—a married way of life. (Since Judge William is Kierkegaard's spokesman for moral life, I will continue to use his masculine exemplar, but this obviously could be just as true of a woman as a man.) This is how the judge sees himself, as one who has overcome the tedium of everydayness by constantly repossessing his first love: "As a true victor, the husband has not killed time but saved and preserved it in eternity. . . . He solves the great riddle: to live in eternity yet so to hear the parlour clock strike" (EO 463).

Conjugal love, the judge goes on to say, "is faithful, constant, humble, patient, forbearing, indulgent, sincere, contented, observant, persistent, willing, joyful. All these virtues have the property of being inward specifications of the individual. The individual does not fight external enemies; it is with itself and its love that it fights it out, of its own accord" (EO 463).

The central concern here is the principle of integrity. This is what the judge is committed to maintaining above all. While he has a great deal to say about family life, children, and maintaining a home, one can hardly overlook the fact that in more than 350 pages of argument there is virtually no reference to his wife. We do not even know her name. This is in sharp contrast to the very sensitive description of Cordelia given by her lover and seducer, Johannes, in volume 1 of *Either/Or*. Kierkegaard has made his point quite effectively: the focus of romantic love is on the personality of the beloved while the focus of moral love is on the integrity of the lover.

We can see why this must be so. The lover's dedication in no way can be contingent upon some particular quality of the beloved — her charm, her nobility of character, or her beauty. What happens when she becomes tiresome or deceitful or less beautiful? Does the lover's dedication vary with each alteration of the beloved? What then becomes of his integrity, his self? It is clear that if the lover is to maintain the constancy of his own identity, his love cannot be dependent on the beloved in any way. In order for his love to be constant, he must be constant in himself.

Even if all of love's duties are not spelled out, there is something substantial about moral love because the self must rely on principle and continuity simply to be a self. There is a kind of concreteness in this. The lover's principles must be repeatedly embodied in visible and tangible acts. His everyday life must be a demonstration. Moreover, unlike romantic love, which defies all reason and understanding, moral love can be understood; it can be translated into language and comprehension because of its consistency. Thus this kind of love has a certain objectivity that can be recognized and respected by others whether or not they choose to emulate it.

The gift of moral love is the gift of the lover's integrity — this is what he freely bestows on his beloved. The duties of love are therefore not extraneous obligations. They are the consequences of the lover's need to be true to himself — to his own choices and principles. Hence, Judge William is right when he argues that the commands of love can be finally decided only by "you yourself" because it is the lover's integrity that is at stake (EO 472). He truly does give himself, but in a way that is paradoxically invulnerable to the variabilities of the beloved.

The "impress of eternity" that moral love bears is not so much the result of carrying out God's commandments as it is due to the loss of meaning if it is not absolute and enduring. In contrast to conditional commitments, which are like contracts (a limited means to a limited end), overarching meaning in life appears only as a consequence of unconditional commitment. What makes love moral is the threat of meaninglessness.

THE ROLE OF REASON

Kant knows perfectly well that love and duty are not the same thing. "Love is a matter of *feeling*, not of *will*," he says, "and I cannot love because I *will* to, still less because I *ought* to (i.e. I cannot be necessitated to love)" (DV 62). Still, even though one cannot be compelled to love, it is nonetheless true that *when* one loves it falls under the a priori conceptions of pure reason. As rational creatures we are governed by the universal laws that pure reason presents to us. We literally have no choice about this. Reason necessarily shows us the ideal — what ought to be. We may not live up to it, we may think it is impractical or hopelessly unrealistic, but we cannot avoid the sense of oughtness (duty) that reason provides to us.

As a lover, for example, I might be inclined to lie in order to seek some particular advantage, but, says Kant, "I can by no means will that lying should be a universal law" (FPMM 20). We know that lying is only advantageous if it is expected to be the truth. If lying were the general practice, what would be the point to it? Indeed, what would lying mean? Pure reason (that is, without any calculation of advantage or disadvantage) shows us that truth-telling is what ought to be. An intentional untruth, even if it does not harm others, is harmful to the teller because it violates his own rational nature. Our sense of duty, in other words, arises necessarily from our capacity to reason consistently. Marvin Fox explains, "A rational creature cannot will the irrational, the inconsistent, the self-contradictory. Moral man is rational man."[9]

For Kierkegaard, however, the factor inherent in human nature that necessitates moral constancy is not reason but rather our capacity for choice. And by this Kierkegaard does not mean merely the choice of one thing or another, or even the choice of good or evil. As he says, it is the far more fundamental kind of choice "whereby one chooses good and evil or excludes them" (EO 486). That is, it is the choice of whether or not to be a moral person. But this is redundant. Like Kant, Kierkegaard seems to be saying that to be moral and to be a person are one and the same thing. The difference is that for Kant this is accomplished by reason, while for Kierkegaard it is essentially a matter of determination, or will, or energy.

In making this kind of basic choice, says Kierkegaard, that "it is less a matter of choosing correctly than of the energy, earnestness and feeling with which one chooses. The personality thereby proclaims itself in its inner infinitude, and the personality is thereby consolidated in turn" (EO 485f). The sovereignty of the self is thus absolute, subordinate neither to reason nor to morality, but the consolidation it presents is only a flimsy facade to conceal the blatant incongruity between its godlike authority and its mundane choices. This absurd contradiction is what the self is. Elsewhere Kierkegaard argues that "man is a synthesis of the infinite and the finite, of the temporal and the eternal, of freedom and necessity." But, of course, such a synthesis is logically impossible. Thus he concludes, "man is not yet a self."[10] This means that selfhood is intrinsically unstable, always on the verge of dissolution, always on the brink of despair. The achievement of integrity, in other words, is never a once and done thing, but must be done again and again.

One must, in fact, "choose despair" because this is the only way that one chooses one's self absolutely, that is, without relying upon reason, tradition, or anything else external to one's original freedom (EO 513). One must not only choose; one must choose to found oneself over and over again. We see, then, why he says the only thing that holds the self together is energy or passionate determination. The very viability of the self depends on commitment that is very nearly desperate.

In both Kant and Kierkegaard we see that the motivation for constancy in a loving relationship originates in human nature. And in both cases we see that loss of meaning is the consequence of logical self-contradiction (Kant) or failure to choose oneself (Kierkegaard). Both are clear that the constancy of love is the source of meaning and value in life.

Kant, in a way, has it easier in that he can rely on the a priori structure of reason that is simply a given in human nature. It does not have to be proven or justified, only acknowledged and obeyed. The disadvantage of this view is that the formality of universal principles appears somewhat distant and even indifferent to human affections. I may, for example, be drawn to another person because of our shared concern about the global environment. But to say that I love him or her because our ecological reasoning is the same seems a bit odd. Intuitively it seems strange to talk of love in such rationalistic terms.

At first glance Kierkegaard's focus on will and commitment appears much closer to what we might ordinarily think moral love would be. But precisely because he does not see any rational sustenance in the self or its loves, there is a fearful despair that underlies his notion of duty. (This is made even more explicit in two subsequent works, *Fear and Trembling* and *Sickness unto Death*.) Absurdity is a constant threat. A man finds that his beloved, the object of his total devotion, is a petty shoplifter. Or, a woman finds that her macho lover likes to wear women's underwear. The disparity between the absoluteness of my commitment and the human frailty of what I am committed to can be overcome only by renewed determination, blind to its effects on others. But if only the energy and power of choice hold the self together with its commitments, what safeguard is there against sheer fanaticism? If I am totally devoted to my beloved, haven't I the right to expect total obedience from him or her? Without the universalizing restraints of reason, a passion this fierce could easily turn into tyranny of some sort.

THE ROLE OF SEXUALITY

In all of Kierkegaard's extensive discussions of love in *Either/ Or* there is very little explicit reference to sexuality as such. In volume 1, eroticism and sensuality are explored as aspects of the "aesthetic," and in volume 2, as we have seen, this entire domain of experience is entirely subordinated to the "ethical" task of consolidating the self in conjugal love. While Judge William makes a few disparaging remarks about "the instant satisfactions" desired by the young aesthete (EO 393), there is little evidence that Kierkegaard sees sex as a problem of physical appetite. It is rather a problem of human freedom, which finds its relation to eternity either in discontinuous "moments" of intense sensibility ("little eternities"), or in the consecrated reduplication of the self in marriage.

Immanuel Kant, on the other hand, in his *Lectures on Ethics*, sees sexual appetite as a serious threat to moral life. By itself and for itself, he says, sexual love "is nothing more than appetite... Taken by itself it is a degradation of human nature" (LE 163). Why? Because sexual appetite makes the other person an "object of enjoyment," that is, merely a means to the achievement of satisfaction.[11] Kant is generally distrustful of the passions because their aim is invariably directed to one's own satisfaction. Sexual inclinations, argues Kant, do not have to do with the whole person, but only with the other's sexual function: "The desire which a man has for a woman is not directed towards her because she is a human being, but because she is a woman" (LE 164). Yielding to such "lusts and inclinations," says Kant, dishonors human nature by "placing it on a level with animal nature" (LE 164). To truly love others is to care for them as whole persons, that is, as rational and moral sovereigns and not merely as sexual creatures. He also notes: "Human love is good-will, affection, promoting the happiness of others and finding joy in their happiness" (LE 163). Sexual desire, as such, leads to none of these and therefore must be brought under the principled relation of whole persons in order to be raised from the animal level and be made fully human.

Thus, one cannot deal with another as if his sexuality were something separable from his rationality and moral freedom. It is the unity of body and soul that constitutes a person and thus it is only in the totality of a fully committed relationship that sexual relations are legitimized (humanized).

As an end in himself, a person may not dispose of himself as a thing (sell himself into slavery, for example), nor may he deal with others as things — slaves, concubines, prostitutes, for example. "The sole condition on which we are free to make use of our sexual desire depends upon the right to dispose over the person as a whole — over the welfare and happiness and generally over all the circumstances of that person" (LE 166f). This right, concludes Kant, is found only in matrimony because only in this relation is it possible for two people to fully surrender their whole persons to each other. In this reciprocal agreement each gets back what is yielded to the other and thus achieves a "unity of will" (LE 167).

Any sexual relation outside of marriage, Kant is saying, is merely
utilitarian—using the other as a thing, a means to an end—and is
therefore profoundly immoral. Anything that compromises the
moral autonomy of another person is wrong—and sex is no
exception to the rule. "If one devotes one's person to another, one
devotes not only sex but the whole person; the two cannot be
separated" (LE 167). If love is to be moral, it is a matter of all or
nothing at all.

The problem in Kant's view is that despite his repeated
insistence on the "whole person," one cannot avoid seeing a basic
duality in his conception of human nature: the rational versus the
appetitive, the moral versus the animal. For Kant, sexuality is
fundamentally alien to being human unless it is brought under the
rule of reason. But this is contrary to our own deepest experience
in which, sometimes at least, our sexuality seems more innate, closer
to our real self, than do the principles of reason. And did we not
see in Plato that even at its most primitive level, there is a
discriminating element in erotic desire? We lust after some things
more than others. Even in our most brutish cravings there is
revealed a selective, choosing, willing power that may or may not
pay any regard to principles or consequences. Sex, in other words,
is just as much mental as it is physical. To try to limit our
understanding of it as merely a physical appetite is to fail to see its
power to pervade the entire personality. Heloise made this
dramatically clear. She was capable of passionately desiring what
was completely contrary to what was good or what was rational
or even what was natural, and yet there was never any doubt as
to her moral sovereignty. She, and she alone, was in charge of her
life. Kant's attempt to identify our "wholeness as persons" with
reason alone is simply not adequate.

What wins our attention in Kant is his stress on the lover as a
sovereign moral consciousness, but he fails to see that this power
of self-transcendence is neither defined by reason nor excluded
from sexuality. Reason may teach us to see the good in terms of a
universal principle, but cannot compel us to do it.

This brings us back to Kierkegaard. With his emphasis on
choice rather than reason he may be closer to seeing the true nature
of sexuality in human experience than Kant is with his division of
the personality. The immense fascination of "The Diary of the
Seducer" in volume 1 of *Either/Or* has little to do with animal

appetite. It has everything to do with the restless consciousness of both the lover and the beloved, coming to ever sharper focus as consummation is approached. We are given no salacious details. The physical aspects are nearly all left to the imagination, yet it is clearly a sexual drama of great intensity. And what makes it exciting is the delicate interaction of the calculating freedom of the seducer with the emergent freedom of his beloved. What he wants, as he repeatedly makes clear, is not merely the satisfaction of animal appetite, but for her to *give* herself—in her freedom—to him (EO 299, 306, 321).

That all of this is manipulative and immoral Kierkegaard makes no attempt to disguise. In fact, the character of the seducer seems deliberately drawn to impress us with both his extraordinary sensitivity and his appalling egoism. The disparity between his sophisticated consciousness and Cordelia's innocent awareness is troubling and confronts us with the close relationship between love and power, an issue that we will see dealt with much more explicitly, but not any more happily, by Jean-Paul Sartre.

For Kierkegaard, who removes himself from the story by means of several pseudonyms, its justification is solely aesthetic, as a sharp contrast to the ethical way of life. The Diary is so artfully crafted, however, that one could never come away from it thinking that sexuality is just an unruly part of our physical makeup. The dramatic intensity of the story makes very clear that sexuality must be understood as issuing from the very core of human personality — freedom itself.

It is precisely because it is of central significance that Kierkegaard in volume 2 makes Judge William weigh in so heavily against a way of life based on such contrived and cavalier choices. Choice, for the judge, is constitutive of the personality. Love, therefore, is not merely a matter of controlling errant appetites but rather is the very fabrication of the self in repeating love's first choice, again and again and again. Sexuality, therefore, is not an issue for the judge because it is simply subsumed as an aspect of this much larger concern.

OUTCOMES

As with Plato, Kant believes that human beings at their best are moved to identify themselves with realities larger than themselves. The difference, however, is that Plato perceives interpersonal love to be a steppingstone that leads us gradually to an ever more inclusive vision, whereas Kant regards interpersonal love as something of an impediment to this goal. Plato's view of erotic love contains within it a discriminating factor (reason, we would say) that escalates the level of desire from the particular to what is more general and qualitatively superior. This is why Plato's dialogues characterize Socrates' erotic interests as having *political* significance.

For Kant, however, reason is not progressive but absolute. Reason is a universal faculty and prescribes duties that extend well beyond personal preferences, fraternal affections, neighborly associations. The rationality of the self cannot in its very nature be limited to a merely private world of exclusive relationships. Every relation to others comes under the thought of pure reason, he notes, and therefore overrides self-seeking inclinations: "I want every other man to be benevolent to me; hence I should also be benevolent to every other man" (DV 118). Principles of fairness and equity and justice actually aim at an ideal society, which requires that our moral responsibilities be carried out with impartial disregard of personal likes and dislikes.

For this reason Kant regards the charm of intimate relations with some suspicion. "Any tendency to close the heart to all but a selected few," he says, "is detrimental to true spiritual goodness, which reaches out after a good-will of universal scope" (LE 206). He concedes that loving friends are a necessity of life, because they help us to correct our judgments and thus help us to enjoy our existence, but this is due to our limited and parochial natures. "The more civilized man becomes, the broader his outlook and the less room there is for special friendships; civilized man seeks universal pleasures and a universal friendship, unrestricted by special ties" (LE 207).

Kierkegaard clearly does not share this enlightenment dream of universal harmony, but because for him the very structure of the self is at stake his moral concern is no less earnest. Love is therefore a serious business. Judge William says, "choosing gives

to a man's nature a solemnity, a quiet dignity, that is never entirely
lost" (EO 490). The passionate otherworldliness of romantic love
can rise to great heights of fancy, but moral love, by contrast, is
very this-worldly and very practical: it tackles head-on the
ordinariness of daily life and transmutes it into steady significance.
As we have seen, it is very inner-directed: it is rooted in the interior
necessity to maintain the wholeness of the self but it is externalized
in the worldly duties that are produced by this inner discipline.
The duties of love, in other words, are an attempt to hold one's
world together, both inner and outer. The preoccupation with
integrity creates an entire way of life, manifested in daily dedication
to the ongoing values of family, career, community, institutions,
social service, and so forth (EO 553).

"It takes work," the advocates of moral love always advise us.
Indeed it does—whether it is the application of rational principles
to the confusions and ambiguities of life (Kant), or whether it is
the reduplication of commitment in the face of tedium and boredom
(Kierkegaard). There is never any suggestion that this is going to
be easy or fun. Pleasure, excitement, intensity are usually
discounted or denied altogether because they are so ephemeral
and distracting. The satisfactions of moral love are found rather
in the enduring coherence of the self—"This is who I am"—and its
objective achievements—"This is what I have made." The judge
even speaks of himself as a "product," a product of his choices
(EO 543).

Ideally, the commitment of the moral lover would be
reciprocated by the beloved and become a joint effort. "Mutual
self-building" is Roger Scruton's very appealing description of this
kind of love: "I identify you as something wholly free, wholly
responsible, all of whose states, including your desire, express the
unspoiled 'self-identity' that is yours. And I seek to attain in your
eyes the same integrity that I attribute to you." What this kind of
love seeks, Scruton goes on to say, is "not a promise of affection,
but a *vow* of loyalty. Vows are more than promises: they involve
the complete surrendering of one's future to a present project, a
solemn declaration that what one now is, one will always be, in
whatever unforeseeable circumstances."[12]

That is, moral love is essentially a task—the task of making
every particular instance, no matter how recalcitrant, into
something continuous and meaningful. "The person who lives

ethically works at becoming the universal man" (EO 547). Moral love is just such a task. It is a "labor of love," one might say, in which a particular individual seeks to transform himself or herself into a universal, a "married man" or a "married woman." This is accomplished not through just one choice (the choice to get married), but through countless subsequent choices that replicate the first choice.

But of course this is impossible, even "absurd" (EO 554). The particular can never be identical with the universal—not logically, not practically. So moral love remains an ongoing task whose "work" never ends. No wonder that Judge William acknowledges (somewhat ruefully, it appears) that ultimately it all depends on energy: "the main thing is still the energy" (EO 544, 557f).

ASSESSMENT

What can we expect of moral love?

What moral love presents to us is an ideal of lofty but paradoxical selflessness. We esteem it so highly because the moral lover has so completely identified himself with constancy and principle. We admire such a person as having rocklike integrity, undeviating in his behavior to the beloved regardless of temptation, misfortune, or changing circumstances. Even faithlessness on the part of the beloved does not deter him, because, at bottom, it is to himself that he is being true. This is the paradox. What ensures the constancy of the moral lover is his absolute commitment to his own integrity; inconstancy would amount to personal disintegration. But the selfless commitment to principle that is so admirable also has the additional ironical effect of being somewhat indifferent to the individuality of the beloved. The particularities of her character, for better or worse, are almost irrelevant. The devotion to principle is "selfless" at both ends of the relationship. That is to say, the strength of the moral lover is also his weakness. He does not listen to temptation, true enough, but neither does he listen to his beloved. In fact, he does not listen very well at all, so preoccupied is he with maintaining his principles, his integrity.

We cannot overlook differences between Kant and Kierkegaard at this point. In the Kantian view, two lovers regard each other as morally autonomous beings, each fully respecting the moral freedom of the other in forming a relationship based on reciprocal rationality. The restraints of reason are the safeguard against any exploitative or deviant inclinations, but of course they also have a certain cooling effect on emotional intimacy. One can expect respect in this view, but not romantic intensity.

The continuity of conjugal love, in Kierkegaard's view, does not so much depend on reason as on inner determination. It may gain something in passion over the Kantian view, but it loses the universalizing safeguard. The lover's commitment to integrity could be the commitment to unyielding patriarchalism, for example. Since the lover's commitment is sustained only by his energy, he need pay no regard to the autonomy of his beloved, but only to maintaining the relationship according to his lights. The difference between love and oppression might be hard to detect in this case.

The danger in both these views, and in the notion of moral love generally, is pride. In both the Kantian and Kierkegaardian version the lover takes a certain satisfaction in his unwavering consistency, in his way of life. He can demonstrate the concreteness of his love in his behavior, in what he has achieved. He can explain its principles and point to its tangible realization. "Look what I have done for you," he is likely to say, ignoring the real truth of the matter—that what he has done has been largely a matter of being true to himself.

Both Kant and Kierkegaard (and Sartre, as we shall see) have the same starting point: an independent "free" self that somehow exists prior to making any choices or reasons or actions—an "isolated I"—and they then try to derive a notion of identity and responsibility from this starting point. In a sense they never get away from it. Their ideas of love actually consist of an extension or projection of the self—the self's principles, the self's choices. But they never really break through the walls of self-containment.

FURTHER READING

There is no single text for Kant's idea of love. The two most accessible sources for his basic views on ethical reasoning are *The Fundamental Principles of the Metaphysics of Morals*, trans. Thomas K. Abbott, with an Introduction by Marvin Fox (New York: Liberal Arts Press, 1949) and his *Lectures on Ethics*, trans. Louis Infeld (New York: Harper Torchbooks, 1963). *The Critique of Practical Reason* is

Kant's great systematic work on the fundamental presuppositions of moral reasoning.

John Kemp's *The Philosophy of Kant* (New York: Oxford University Press, 1968) provides a good overall introduction to Kant's work. Roger Scruton's *Sexual Desire – A Moral Philosophy of the Erotic* (New York: Free Press, Macmillan, 1986) is a contemporary conservative view that follows Kantian lines of argument on the problem of love.

For readers with big appetites, there is no better introduction to the thought of Søren Kierkegaard than his first main work (1843), *Either/Or*, parts 1 and 2, trans. and ed. Howard V. Hong and Edna H. Hong (Princeton: Princeton University Press, 1987). For greater accessibility to readers the references in this discussion are from an abridged translation by Alastair Hannay: *Either/Or – A Fragment of Life* (New York: Penguin Books, 1992).

Two slimmer works, *Fear and Trembling* and *Repetition*, ed. and trans. Howard V. Hong and Edna V. Hong (Princeton: Princeton University Press, 1983), are recommended, although not easy reading. Kierkegaard's major work is *Concluding Unscientific Postscript*, trans. David P. Swenson and Walter Lowrie (Princeton: Princeton University Press, 1944).

A very handy collection of selections from Kierkegaard's major works is *A Kierkegaard Anthology*, ed. Robert Bretall (New York: Modern Library, Random House, 1936).

Patrick Gardiner's *Kierkegaard* (Oxford: Oxford University Press, 1988) is a helpful general introduction to the significance of this Danish philosopher.

NOTES

1. Immanuel Kant, *Fundamental Principles of the Metaphysics of Morals*, trans. T. K. Abbott (New York: Liberal Arts Press, 1949), p.25. Hereafter designated in the text as FPMM.

2. Kant: "Freedom of choice is this independence from sensuous impulse in the determination of choice." *Doctrine of Virtue*, part 2 of the *Metaphysics of Morals*, trans. Mary J. Gregor (Philadelphia: University of Pennsylvania Press, 1964), p. 10. Hereafter designated in the text as DV.

3. "The positive concept of freedom is that of power of pure reason to be of itself practical. But pure reason can be practical only if the maxim of every action is subjected to the condition that it qualifies as a universal law." Kant, *Doctrine of Virtue*, p. 10.

4. Mary J. Gregor, *Laws of Freedom* (Oxford: Basil Blackwell, 1963), p. 184.

5. Carol Gilligan, *In a Different Voice: Psychological Theory and Woman's Development* (Cambridge, Mass.: Harvard University Press, 1982).

6. Henry David Aiken, *Reason and Conduct – New Bearings in Moral Philosophy* (New York: Alfred Knopf, 1962), pp. 82, 104.

7. Immanuel Kant, *Lectures on Ethics*, trans. L. Infield (London: Methuen & Co., 1930), pp. 202f. Hereafter designated in the text as LE.

8. Søren Kierkegaard, *Either/Or – A Fragment of Life*, abr. and trans. Alastair Hannay (London: Penguin Books, 1992), p. 432. Hereafter designated in the text as EO.

9. Marvin Fox, Introduction, Kant, *Fundamental Principles of the Metaphysics of Morals*, p. xv.

10. Søren Kierkegaard, *Fear and Trembling & Sickness unto Death*, trans. W. Lowrie (Garden City, N.Y.: Doubleday Anchor, 1954), p. 146.

11. "It [sex] is rather pleasure from the *use* of another person, which therefore belongs to the appetitive power and, indeed, to the *appetitive* power in its highest degree, passion." Kant, *Doctrine of Virtue*, p. 90.

12. Roger Scruton, *Sexual Desire – A Moral Philosophy of the Erotic* (New York: Free Press, Macmillan, 1986), p. 242.

Chapter 6

ℵ

LOVE AS POWER: THOMAS HOBBES, G.W.F. HEGEL AND JEAN-PAUL SARTRE

Hunger allows no choice
To the citizen or the police;
We must love one another or die.

—W. H. Auden

"All's fair in love and war," it is commonly said. The analogy between love and war is at first unsettling, but on reflection we realize there is some truth in it. Love can be as all-encompassing and absolutely ruthless as war. Lovers do sometimes behave as if their very being were at stake. When this happens moral concerns are shrugged aside or suspended. The struggle for love seems so much more urgent and vital that goodness appears trivial by comparison.

Instead of raising people to a higher level of moral concern, love can have quite the opposite effect—a return to the mentality of Thomas Hobbes's primordial state of nature in which savage self-interest is uppermost.[1] Writing in the seventeenth century, Hobbes tried to establish the basis of civil life by making a tough-minded assessment of the hard facts of human nature. Fear and desire are what rule us, he observed. We call "good" those things that we desire, and those things that inspire fear and aversion we call "evil."[2] Mutual respect, principled relations, constancy, and consistency are thus all quite irrelevant. What matters most is our pleasure and our security: how to get what we want and how to keep what we get. To use Hobbes's words, it is like "a time of war, where every man is enemy to every man."[3]

How can love lead people to behave like this?

In Hobbes's view the reason why every man is the enemy of every other man is that each person, no matter how weak, has the power to take the life of another person. Cunning and stealth make us all equal in this respect.[4] Thus, from the moment of birth, each person seeks by whatever means to make his or her insecure existence as secure as possible. The struggle for power originates in human vulnerability. This life and death struggle at the very basis of human existence makes government a necessity in order to restrain us from each other. Without this implied social contract civilized life would be impossible. Deep down, though, we all know that if anyone were really determined enough, he could take the life of another. Hobbes exposed the dark secret of human society: we literally have the power of life and death over each other.

Similarly, we recognize our vulnerability in love. If my beloved does indeed "mean everything" to me, then I am in fact in thrall to him. He could extinguish my life, or at least its meaning, by withdrawing his love. By loving him, I have given him power over me. I am in a double bind: I need him, yet he is a threat to me. Love itself becomes something to be feared because of how vulnerable I become. Or, alternately, I may think that by loving him I have power over him. Love justifies all. A Hobbesian might well argue that at bottom what we desire most intensely is love and what we fear most seriously is the loss of love. Hence, love is like war in that it is the struggle for something even as important as life itself.

But Hobbes is not alone in finding struggle at the very basis of human existence. A little less than two centuries later, another philosopher, Georg Wilhelm Friedrich Hegel, showed that conflict was not simply a political fact of life but was inherent in the very nature of human consciousness itself. It is worth examining what Hegel says in this regard, because his analysis lays the groundwork for Jean-Paul Sartre's idea of love, which will be the focus of this discussion of love as power. What Hegel says about the conflicted way the *mind* works provides the pattern for Sartre's view of the way *love* works.

Consciousness is inherently divided against itself, says Hegel. Consciousness cannot grasp itself; it must always grasp something *other* than itself. I cannot just think (or feel); I must think (or feel) something. Moreover, every thought or feeling can also be thought to be otherwise, or even not to be at all. That is to say, consciousness contains within itself its own negation or contradiction. I am not only aware, I am aware that things could be otherwise. My awareness of hunger, for example, is in contrast to my previous sense of satisfaction. The difference between these two is what Hegel calls "desire." Moreover, when I am hungry I realize that *I* am the one who has the desire for food. Thus, in desire I (reflexively) become aware of myself. The fact that awareness is not identical with itself, but desires something *other* is what produces self-consciousness — that is, the consciousness of our consciousness. "Self-consciousness is *desire*," says Hegel.[5]

There are, then, two opposed forms or modes of consciousness, says Hegel: "The one is independent, and its essential nature is to be for itself; the other is dependent, and its essential nature is life or existence for another." That is, in one mode consciousness affirms itself (it is what it is) and in its other mode makes a negation (it could be otherwise) that depends on the initial assertion. Hegel personifies these two modes by calling the former, "master," and the latter, "bondsman" (or "servant").[6]

Remember that what we are talking about is the mental process by which we (as subjects) come to have knowledge of things (as objects) and of ourselves (as both subjects and objects). To be a subject *requires* us to have objects. Hegel's point is that this process evolves from a very fundamental conflict within itself — between the "master" mode of consciousness and the "servant" mode. Thus, self-consciousness exists both for-itself and in-itself, as both independent and dependent, and they are linked by desire. Each mode of consciousness depends on the other for its existence and yet each seeks to obliterate the other to demonstrate its self-certainty. "Consciousness finds that it immediately is and is not another consciousness, as also that this other is for itself only when it cancels itself as existing for itself, and has self-existence only in the self-existence of the other."[7]

Hegel shows us that how we come to know anything is the result of this split within our own mental processes. The first step is the knower's differentiation between himself and what he knows.

It is an internal negation. When I see a pencil the first distinction I make is that the pencil is *not* me. To be a subject is not to be an object, and to be an object is to be negated by a subject. Consciousness, in other words, must be mediated through opposition, through otherness. The sharper the negation, the clearer is our knowledge of objects and, also, the clearer is our self-awareness. Within consciousness, therefore, these two modes — "master" and "servant" — are locked in a life and death struggle. "They must enter this struggle," Hegel goes on to say, "for they must bring their certainty of themselves, the certainty of being for themselves, to the level of objective truth."[8]

What Hegel is discussing here are modes of consciousness, but he personifies each mode to make us see them in terms of human behavior. Recognition is what each mode (and person) seeks above all — recognition from the other of its freedom, "and it is solely by risking life that freedom is obtained." The full power of self-consciousness, in other words, requires recognition from another that he will risk everything, even life itself, to prove that he is absolutely independent: "The individual who has not staked his life may, no doubt, be recognized as a person; but he has not attained the truth of this recognition as an independent self-consciousness."[9] The one who stops short of the ultimate risk — the one who blinks — becomes the servant. The one who has demonstrated his freedom by risking his very being becomes the master. Even in this victory, however, the master paradoxically becomes the loser because his independence is only recognized by a dependent being (the servant) who must do his bidding. The full recognition that the master seeks could only come from another consciousness as independent as he is — and this he cannot tolerate. The struggle would start all over again.

Hegel's parable of the two modes of consciousness as "master and servant" is so vivid that we are tempted to forget that what he is talking about is essentially a phenomenology of mind — an account of the relation of subject and object in the process of knowing. What the parable shows us is that consciousness is the result of conflict — the conflict between our need for opposition (we must have it in order to be sure of who we are, or even that we are) and the necessity to overcome that opposition in order to prove the independence of consciousness. For Hegel the inner contradictions of this "unhappy consciousness"[10] are ultimately reconciled in a more comprehensive and progressive view of human history. For Jean-Paul Sartre, however, this is not merely an insight about the way consciousness works, but a profound intuition about the conflicted nature of our very being.[11]

THE DEFINING RELATION

The power of negation, which Hegel found to be central to self-*consciousness*, is taken by Sartre to be the central fact of human *existence*. Sartre argues that our capacity to conceive the contrary of any state of affairs means that we are essentially indeterminate beings. Freedom is virtually the same thing as the power to conceive negatively. This means that when we act, we are responsible for our actions because we could conceive of having done otherwise. "My consciousness sticks to my acts, it is my acts," says Sartre (BN348). Nothing compels us to act in a particular way. We are our actions because they are our choices.

The preeminent characteristic of human existence, therefore, is that it lacks substance. The self, in and of itself, is nothing. I am a center of freedom that can negate anything and everything, even my own past. Does this mean that I can do anything I want? That I can ignore the physical, social, and economic forces that determine the world? No, the power of negation that constitutes my essential freedom is the power of consciousness, but this is not the same as power over the material world. It is rather the power to determine the meaning and value of *my* world. Certain kinds of hard facts may be out of my control, but their significance is the result of my choices. And even the so-called hard facts can be transformed by my interpretation of them, by my plans and projects, by what I make out of them. There is no fact, no matter how distasteful, that can determine whatever choice I make about it. No fact can make me do anything. I can always say no, even if death is the consequence.

But this uniquely human power of negation means that there is a split at the heart of human existence. We are never fully at one with ourselves. Everything that we are aware of can be conceived of otherwise. We can conceive of having different bodies, of being richer, of being more successful, of having made other choices, of living altogether differently. Not that we can or will do any of these things—but my sense of self, my "I," is other than any fixed

thing about me. To be conscious *of* something, even something
about myself, is *not* to be that thing. In other words, my
consciousness is essentially my freedom. I am conscious of things —
physical objects (including my own body), mental objects (such as
mathematical concepts or historical facts), and I am certainly
conscious of other people's ideas about me. But I am not reducible
to any of these things or even to any combination of them.

At the same time, however, my self-awareness is to some
considerable extent derived from my awareness of others. My
choices may be my own, but those actions are described,
categorized, and evaluated by others. My freedom is transmuted
into the perceptions of others. I may have had certain intentions
in acting but the characterizations of those actions are made by
others and may be quite different from what I had in mind. For
better or for worse I am confronted with an image of myself derived
from others. Even if I attempt to provide my own account of my
acts, I am unavoidably dependent on others' language and values
to do so: "The Other is the indispensable mediator between myself
and me." If I do something stupid or vulgar, it has no significance
unless someone sees me. But when I am observed, "I am ashamed
of myself *as I appear* to the Other....I recognize that I *am* as the
Other sees me" (BN302).

On the one hand, therefore, "I am my acts," as Sartre says
(BN347), but, at the same time, I am alienated from my acts in at
least two ways. First of all, I am not my acts in the sense that my
freedom is always other than what I have done. I may have studied
hard to pass a certain course, but I could decide at the last moment
not to take the final exam. Nothing requires me to identify myself
with my previous actions. I can disown them. Second, I am not
my acts in the sense that I do not control others' perceptions of
them. My decision to drop out of school may be seen by some as
an act of independence, while others may regard my decision as
reckless and irresponsible. In either case there is an "other" within
my own sense of self. My dependence on the other in my being
was "Hegel's brilliant intuition," says Sartre: "I am, he said, a
being for-itself which is for-itself only through another. Therefore
the Other penetrates me to the heart" (BN321).

The conflict within ourselves, between our acts and our
negation of them, is thus magnified in our relations to others. We
are defenseless, even enslaved, by the freedom of others to see and

evaluate and judge us as they please. "I am a slave to the degree that my being is dependent at the very center of a freedom which is not mine and which is the very condition of my being" (BN358). One of the characters in Sartre's play *No Exit* comes to realize, "Hell is other people!"[12] The most agonizing torment imaginable is not a fire-and-brimstone torture chamber, but being tied inextricably to the regard of others for our very being.

In many ways, of course, we suppress this conflict in order to win the goodwill of others. It would be very difficult to function in the middle-class world, for example, if we were not regarded as law-abiding and responsible citizens. A successful business or professional career requires building up a reputation for honesty and reliability. We may, however, find ourselves defined in the eyes of others in ways that make us very uncomfortable but that we cannot altogether reject. A business person, for example, may offer certain product lines that reveal his essential concern to be the profit motive and not the welfare of his customers as he advertises himself.

Sartre gives a very dramatic example of losing control over one's identity and self-image. He tells of a man who is secretly observing another person by peeping through a keyhole. He is wholly absorbed in what he is doing. But when he suddenly hears someone behind him and realizes that he has been seen by someone else, he is embarrassed as he becomes aware of himself as seen through the eyes of another. In a sense, he has lost control of his self to the freedom of another person. He is "transcendence transcended," says Sartre. His power to make the person he was observing into an object has been overcome by the one who has observed *him*. He is now the object of another's observation. He is now a "voyeur" — something categorized and judged by the one who has seen him peeping at another (BN347–349).

This epitomizes our relations with others. Each encounter with another is the attempt of my freedom to surmount the freedom of the other, to make that person an object of my valuations and intentions; and simultaneously, the other person is attempting to do the same thing with me. "While I attempt to free myself from the hold of the Other, the Other is trying to free himself from mine; while I seek to enslave the Other, the Other seeks to enslave me....Conflict is the original meaning of being-for-others" (BN474f). Thus, all human relationships are essentially power struggles. I must have the recognition of others to be a self—if no one paid any attention to what I did, my freedom would be pointless—but I must be recognized as a "master" and not as a "servant."

While Sartre's analysis shows this struggle to be inherent in all human relationships, some are obviously more important than others. If, like the peeping tom, for example, I were caught in the act by a stranger it would be mildly embarrassing but could be shrugged off as fairly insignificant. But if I were caught by someone whose regard was very important to me, say, my beloved, then it would be extremely damaging to my self-esteem. "The value of the Other's recognition of me depends on the value of my recognition of the Other" (BN320). Only in a few relationships do we feel the totality of the self is put on the line. This is why the experience of love is so important. When I love someone I confer upon him or her the power of my self-recognition. I become hostage to that person's view of me, but at the same time I do everything I can to control that view.

This is what love is, an attempt to get the other to see that "I am everything" to him or her, that is, that I am in total possession of his or her freedom. This is the defining relation: the beloved is the other whose freedom I seek to possess, says Sartre, because he "holds a secret—the secret of what I am." He sees me as I can never see myself. "He makes me be and thereby he possesses me." I lose myself in the perceptions of others whom I cannot control, but his recognition gives me being. "By virtue of consciousness the Other is for me simultaneously the one who has stolen my being from me and the one who causes 'there to be' a being which is my being" (BN475). Only through his eyes do I see myself. In this sense, then, love is the attempt to recover my being through capturing the beloved's freedom.

THE ROLE OF REASON

In our discussion of moral love we found constancy, consistency, and principled behavior to be of the uppermost value. One of the appealing things about moral love is that it can be translated to language and can be explained. One's actions can be justified. But understanding love as power turns us 180 degrees in the opposite direction. Like Hobbes, Sartre does not believe that morality has any rational basis. Reason does not determine our behavior. Reason takes a back seat to the power of negation, to the power of choice. Reasons are the consequences of choice, not its foundation.

Therefore, any attempt to justify oneself by appeal to law, moral codes, cultural values, or the like, are forms of what Sartre calls "bad faith," because they all are attempts to escape one's essential freedom. "My freedom is the unique foundation of values and that nothing, absolutely nothing, justifies me in adopting this or that particular value, this or that particular scale of values. As a being by whom values exist, I am unjustifiable" (BN76). If the self is essentially the power of negation—the radical freedom not to be any kind of a thing, not even a moral thing—then the only support for values in the world is my freedom, my choices. "It is I who sustain values in being," says Sartre, "without justification and without excuse" (BN77–78).

Bad faith consists basically in pretending that we are not free. It is a disease of consciousness, one might say, that is demonstrated whenever we present ourselves as being without the power of negation. So as citizen, or teacher, or husband I justify myself by saying that I had to obey the law, I had to assign the homework, I had to bring my wife flowers—as if I had no choice to do otherwise. The most serious thing about bad faith is not merely the attempt to conceal our freedom from others, but our own self-deception. Bad faith is lack of authenticity, insincerity, phoniness. In effect, our freedom is employed to deny our freedom, to evade the responsibility of seeing that nothing determines our acts but our own choices. Bad faith is the pretense, to ourselves as well as to others, that we are objects—something determined, without freedom and without choice.

The very thing, then, that we must do in order to be perceived as responsible members of society—that is, to dedicate ourselves to certain functions that we carry out consistently and energetically—is precisely what Sartre calls "bad faith." Not only must we take on certain social or professional roles, but we must convince everyone that we will not deviate from them. Who would trust a scientist or a doctor or a government official who only seemed to be "playing" his role, like an actor, and was not totally identified with it? Certainly not the public, certainly not his superiors. Even sincerity itself, therefore, can be a form of bad faith. Not only must we behave in a completely functionalized way, as if we wholly lacked freedom, but we must convince ourselves that this is genuine. Reason is little more than rationalization.

From this point of view, therefore, moral life is not an achievement but an escape, a flight from freedom. To live a life of adherence to principle is actually a denial of one's responsibility for each moment—a refusal to face each situation with the full realization of one's freedom to act. Constancy, continuity, devotion to duty, and so forth, are all merely rationalized forms of evasion.

THE ROLE OF SEXUALITY

The key to this entire understanding of love as power is to be found, as we have seen, in Sartre's appropriation of Hegel's analysis of consciousness. The difference is that for Hegel the master-servant parable portrays the underlying logic of the development of knowledge (the logic of objectification), while for Sartre it reveals the underlying and unavoidable reality of conflict in our relations with others.

Love is a subset of the larger problem of our ambiguous relations with others. Love matters so much because it defines the most important relationship through which I seek to have my individuality recognized and to possess the freedom of the other who recognizes it. But my dream of union with the other is an illusion because she cannot be simultaneously an independent reflection of my freedom and dependent on my freedom. She cannot be both subject and object, and yet this contradiction is precisely what love seeks.

Nowhere is this ambiguity more apparent than in sexual experience; yet we are often tempted to simplify sexuality as mainly a problem having to do with our physical nature. But, again, it is the logic of objectification brought to life. The crucial issue is the extent to which my body and the body of the other are the manifestations of subjectivity, of freedom. In some modes my body is thinglike, an object, but in other modes it is the fullest expression of my subjectivity and freedom.

My body is purely object, for example, to the examination of a doctor, and even to myself when I regard it anatomically as bones, muscles, glands, and so on. But there is another sense in which my body is not merely an object but is my way of being in the world—it is the concrete way in which I walk, see, sit in a chair, reach for things on a shelf, and so forth. It constitutes both the limits and possibilities of my practical involvement in the world.

There is still another sense in which my body can be the incorporation of my subjectivity in the eyes of another. We are not ashamed of our own nakedness, for example, but we are embarrassed at being seen naked by another. In this sense I am possessed by the other: "The Other's look fashions my body in its nakedness, causes it to be born, sculptures it, produces it as it is, sees it as I shall never see it" (BN475). My embarrassment is evidence that I have been objectified by another's subjective regard.

Suppose, however, that the nakedness was intentional, a deliberate act calculated to arouse the erotic interest of the other. In this case my body is the means by which I seek to capture the subjectivity of the other. The difference is desire. "In desire," says Sartre, "I make myself flesh in the presence of the Other in order to appropriate the Other's flesh" (BN506). A kind of "clogging of consciousness" thus takes place in lovemaking. Each seeks to incarnate the other's subjectivity as fully as possible in his or her body.

Every aspect of my physical being now becomes the vehicle for my consciousness—how I talk, how I look, how I move—all in an attempt to evoke the presence of the other in her flesh. Similarly, every nuance of her behavior becomes charged with significance as she seeks to do the same with me. Desire aims at mutual incarnation. This is enchantment (BN511).

Sartre's extremely acute analysis makes clear that what makes sexual activity exciting is not the physical aspect as such. The touch of skin upon skin is not intrinsically interesting—as when we are examined by a doctor, for example. It is the attention of a *particular* person that we want. What makes her touch exciting is when it is the disclosure of her intention—her desire, her subjectivity. My desire is not simply for her body but for her desire. My focus on her is to bring her spirit to the surface—to totally engage her freedom with her body: "The caress does not want simple *contact*...the caress is not a simple stroking; it is a *shaping*. In caressing the Other I cause her flesh to be born beneath my caress, under my fingers. The caress is the ensemble of those rituals which *incarnate* the Other" (BN506f).

So it is not just the other's body that I want. Plato and Kant are wrong to equate sexual desire with appetites: flesh is not the object of my desire. What I want is to ensnare the other's freedom within the objective facticity of her body—it "must come to play on the surface of her body, and be extended all through her body; and by touching this body I should finally touch the Other's free subjectivity." It is her real presence that I want. Yes, I want to "possess" her body, but only insofar as she is identified with it (BN511–512). Otherwise she would have eluded me.

The breakdown of mutual incarnation is of course inevitable—it is at best a mutual illusion. I can summon the appearance of the other's freedom in her flesh, but I cannot possess it. I can show my own freedom in my actions, but I cannot give it away. The "isolated I" remains the isolated I. The breakdown thus moves either in the direction of masochism or sadism. In an attempt to save the relationship I may seek to become the object of the other in order to keep her love. By submitting to her and willingly enduring suffering, I attempt to give significance to my life because it is *for* her. What this reveals is the failure of masochism, Sartre points out, because in fact what I am doing is using the other in a (perverse) way to give my life meaning. Despite appearances to the contrary, she is the one whose transcendence is transcended. The fundamental freedom that constitutes subjectivity cannot in the last analysis be denied. Even the attempt to deny freedom is in fact an affirmation of it.

Just as masochism is the perverse result of denying my own freedom, so sadism is the perverse result of denying the freedom of the other by trying to compel her identification with her body. The use of pain and violence are attempts to force the body to invade consciousness. The point, however, is not simply to inflict pain— it is not punishment. Success for the sadist is the moment when the victim reveals herself in her anguish. Sadism is like love in that it seeks incarnation: "What the sadist thus so tenaciously seeks…is the Other's freedom" as it is disclosed by her body (BN522f). But the success of this can only be momentary at best. Moreover, as long as the victim is conscious there is always the possibility that she can turn the tables on the sadist and make *him* into an object through her ridicule or glance of contempt.

The ways in which power defines the sexual relation has been a latent issue beginning with our discussion of erotic love. We saw how the tension between Socrates and Alcibiades exemplifies an erotic game in which sexuality is a struggle for mastery—over oneself, over others—and this preoccupation recurs again in the Christian view, the romantic view, and the moral view of love, Kierkegaard's "Diary of the Seducer" being perhaps the modern analogue to the erotic duet of Socrates and Alcibiades. "The quest for power" is a central issue in modern Western thinking (Hobbes and Descartes, are examples),[13] and it surfaces again in Hegel's master-servant parable, which is his attempt to give a logical characterization to the problematic sovereignty of the self.

But what if the self is not sovereign? What if power emanates not from the freedom of the self but from some more comprehensive reality in which the self is situated? Hegel thought that human passions were ultimately governed by historical objectivity. Marx turned the process upside down and argued that economic and social forces were actually what produced meanings and choices. More recently, Michel Foucault has maintained that the whole domain of sexual relations (as well as everything else) is defined and valorized by "powers" far transcending individuals that are neither as structured nor as rational as Hegel and Marx thought.[14] Following in the footsteps of Nietzsche's assertion that human behavior is motivated, at bottom, by the "will-to-power," Foucault argues that all social relations are "force relations" and are thus embedded in language, law, social practices, and cultural values. These powers are intelligible but not orderly in any comprehensive sense. Examples might be the reigning but ever-shifting ideas of "health" and "illness," "pleasure" and "work," that prevail in any given community. They are "moving substrates" that are local, multiple, and without any overall purpose or reason. They are not expressions of mind, as Hegel might say, nor are they products of economic forces, as Marx might say. Nor can they be understood simplistically as external to individuals, as in repressive institutions or dominating authorities. Rather, these power relations serve as a "general matrix" for life and hence are immanent within individual choices and decisions.[15] In ancient Greek ethics, for example, "standards of sexual morality were always tailored to one's way of life, which was itself determined by the status one had inherited and the purposes one had chosen."[16] Those in public life, especially, imposed rigorous standards on themselves in order to show their superior authority.

By such arguments, Foucault undercuts Sartre's fundamental assumption that the power to determine meaning lies within the freedom of the self. In Foucault's view, the struggle of one subjectivity to find itself in another subjectivity would be only an epiphenomenon—an instance where the intersection of certain codes and values establishes meaning.

Foucault observes, therefore, that the disciplined nature of erotic love that we noted in our discussion of the *Symposium* was not so much the consequence of the pursuit of beauty and truth, but rather the effect of an upper-class ethos—"a principle of stylization of conduct for those who wished to give their existence the most graceful and accomplished form possible."[17] What is at work here, in other words, is a certain aesthetic sense, held by the elite, which requires moderation and restraint in order to achieve "the purposeful art of a freedom perceived as a power game."[18] One can still say that love is power, but this is not one center of freedom grappling with another. It is decentered power in which the significance of subjectivity has been absorbed by larger realms of discourse that establish the "truth" of what takes place between persons. From Foucault's "bird's-eye view" (as he puts it) this makes a certain sense. But from such a distance passions are merely social performances.

Within the realm of lived experience one does not have the advantage of this kind of distance. When one is in love the immediacy of the other fills the entire field of vision. We do not confront "powers" or "force relations" in the actuality of lived experience. They are abstractions. Desire as I actually experience it is evoked only by an other who has the power to recognize me as freedom.

OUTCOMES

Sartre's analysis reveals something of the inner necessity that pushes us into love as no other idea does. As he says, the self is essentially isolated in its freedom (BN60). Because its absolute freedom is absolute nothingness, we have no choice but to be lovers: since we are nothing in ourselves, we *must* find ourselves in another. A little like Plato, Sartre shows us that since the self lacks being it is inevitably driven to the other in an attempt to gain a substantiality it does not have in itself. Unlike Plato, however, what the self gets is not greater permanence and ideality, but only the fleeting recognition achieved by conquest of or surrender to the freedom of the other.

One of the reasons love is so alluring is that it seems to offer a foundation for our lives. Unable to justify ourselves, we look to our beloved to provide us with a reason for living. "She (or he) means everything to me," lovers say. But how can the foundation of my life depend upon the possession of another's freedom? It is a mutual contradiction. In Sartre's hands the paradox of love emerges in full force. What Hegel describes as alternating modes of consciousness in his master-servant parable becomes for Sartre the paradigm of irresolvable conflict between lovers. To find myself in another is to require either my surrender or that of my beloved. Since the freedom of each is untransferable, love is fundamentally contradictory and doomed to failure. Roger Scruton notes, "Love requires the total surrender of what is totally free, and absolute unity between what is utterly diverse."[19]

The complexities raised by this view are considerable. For one thing, the ostensible aim of the lover is in principle self-contradictory. The lover seeks to recover his being by totally absorbing the freedom of the other, but if he is successful in this, the beloved is no longer "other." The beloved would no longer be separate enough to provide the sense of distinct identity that the self craves. In other words, if love achieves unity, it fails.

This leads us back to the dilemma posed by Hegel's master-servant parable. What love seeks is the other's freedom — the totality of the beloved's consciousness. The lover does not want merely an inert thing, an object. Nor does he want her out of fear or compulsion or even duty. Recognition given by a slave does not amount to much. Nor is love very satisfying if given by one who is dependent or bound by obligation. It is "freedom as freedom" that the lover wants to possess (BN478). But, of course, the moment this freedom is surrendered — "Take me, I'm yours!" — it is no longer freedom. At the very moment of triumph, the self as lover loses what he wants — the free recognition of himself by another. What the self really seems to want, says Sartre, is that the beloved should somehow "will its own captivity" so that the love given is both free and yet securely possessed by the lover (BN479).

But there are still further complications. How is the lover to get the beloved to surrender her freedom? Tactics of domination and control are obviously self-defeating. What he must do is to somehow make himself an object of her desire. She must want him to be "all the world" to her and so he must fashion himself into being her world. That is, in loving her, what he really wants is for her to love him. He must present himself to her as one to whom she would want to give her freedom. And she, on her part, must present herself in such a way that he would want her to want him to want her to love him . . . and so on. The infinite regress here is dizzying but does in fact seem to characterize the insecurity of most love affairs. Love is this endlessly shifting reciprocity of two freedoms, each trying to capture the other without being captured, as uncertain and confusing as a game of hide-and-seek in a hall of mirrors. No wonder that Sartre says that love is essentially conflict and that a truly satisfying love affair is impossible.

ASSESSMENT

What can we expect from love as power?

More than any other view this concept of love illumines the complexities and uncertainties that confound every loving relationship. By lifting the veil of sentimentality, we see that what is really going on is a power struggle, and we see now why the struggle is so desperate. Our very being as persons is at stake: it is either "being or nothingness" — one might say. Or at least it seems that way from inside the experience of love as it is lived from day to day. Now we see why fairly trivial incidents can be so emotionally explosive; now we see why subtle gestures can be so exciting or so disappointing. The power that love seeks is the power of recognition, both of myself and of the beloved. Love is risky business — it confers upon another the power to make or break me.

This also explains why those outside the relationship do not really understand what is going on. "No one knows what's in the pot except the spoon that stirs it," says the Spanish proverb. Only from within my lived experience can I know whether my freedom has triumphed — or hers.

This shows how both the strength and weakness of this idea of love stem from its dependence on Hegel's analysis of consciousness. As an account of our interior awareness it is accurate: mentally we can in fact negate anything and everything. Sartre's descriptions of the fluidity of consciousness reveal how freely our attentions and intentions slip from one thing to another, quite independent of logic, moral constraints, or realistic limitations of any kind. This gives rise to an illusion of absolute freedom and absolute responsibility.

But the world "out there" — the exterior world — is not so negatable. There are intractable facts such as birth, death, physical limitations, and so forth. True, none of these facts can necessarily determine my attitude or what I will do about them, but they do have hard, deterministic connections with each other — babies have to be fed and cared for, crops cannot be harvested if they are not planted, water pipes freeze at thirty-two degrees Fahrenheit, the rent has to be paid.

So in love affairs, I may in principle be aware of my power to negate the other (assert my freedom), but in practice the entanglements of time and nature are such that they are inescapable. The sovereignty of my interior self may be absolute, but the freedom of my lived experience is so constrained as to be noticeable only at the margins.

While Sartre's analysis goes far toward explaining why love can be so exciting and threatening and exasperating, it does not adequately come to grips with love in the real world "out there." In principle, yes, I can negatively conceive virtually anything, but in practice, as we all know, this is extremely difficult, if not impossible. Traditions, circumstances, family and peer pressures, moral authorities — all weigh heavily upon us. They confront us like tangible realities. The fact that they cannot be readily denied makes very clear the extent to which I am identified with them, often without choosing to do so — family, for example. My consciousness is just free enough to recognize them as powers outside myself, but not free enough to overcome them. Even if I do manage to transcend them momentarily I know perfectly well that they will outlast me and that I cannot get rid of them once and for all.

Sartre himself observes in an earlier essay, "What does not vary is the necessity to exist in the world, to be at work there, to be there in the midst of other people, and to be mortal there."[20] Similarly, it is "in the world" where love takes place. It is not merely a matter of interior consciousness, of a radically free for-itself. Love is a matter of engagements with others who resist us, disappoint us, surprise us, make demands on us — and sometimes support us.

Maybe this is not a bad thing. If love were solely a function of consciousness, it might very well be the failure that Sartre says it is. But because love is a matter of concrete actions and material involvement, it acquires a continuity and permanence that consciousness never has. As we have seen, desire aims at incarnation, and materialized love acquires a certain stability. It cannot be disengaged quite as freely as consciousness. Love in the real world may succeed despite the logic of consciousness.

FURTHER READING

Jean-Paul Sartre's first major philosophical work (1943), and the basis for most of the discussion in this chapter, is *Being and Nothingness*, trans. Hazel E. Barnes (New York: Washington Square Press, Pocket Books, 1956). A massive work, it presumes familiarity with European philosophers such as Descartes, Hegel, Husserl, and Heidegger. Even though some parts are very dense, the reader would be rewarded by some of the investigations of lived experience ("Bad Faith," for example, and "Concrete Relations with Others") that made Sartre the center of much philosophical controversy in the period following World War II. As much a literary figure as a philosopher, his sense of life as action and decision was given dramatic expression in novels, short stories, and plays. Some of his key ideas are made quite accessible in *No Exit and Three Other Plays*, trans. Stuart Gilbert (New York: Vintage Books, 1955). A brief and readable introduction to Sartre's thinking is *Existentialism*, tr. Bernard Frechtman (New York: Philosophical Library, 1947), a popular lecture that he gave in 1945, although he later repudiated its implications for establishing humanistic ethics.

An excellent overall discussion and critical review of Sartre's work is provided by Wilfrid Desan's *The Tragic Finale – An Essay on the Philosophy of Jean-Paul Sartre* (New York: Harper Torchbooks, Harper & Row, 1960).

NOTES

1. Thomas Hobbes, *Leviathan* (New York: Collier Macmillan, 1962). See especially chapter 13, "Of the Natural Condition of Mankind," pp. 98–102.

2. Ibid., pp. 47–48.

3. Ibid., p. 100.

4. Ibid., pp. 98f.

5. G.W.F. Hegel, *The Phenomenology of Mind*, trans. J. B. Baillie (New York: Harper Torchbook, 1967), p. 225.

6. Ibid., p. 234. Hegel's terms are *Herr* and *Knecht,* which seem more appropriately translated as "Master" and "Servant" than as "Lord" and "Bondsman."

7. Ibid., p. 231.

8. Ibid., p. 232.

9. Ibid., p. 233.

10. Ibid., p. 251.

11. Jean-Paul Sartre, *Being and Nothingness*, trans. Hazel E. Barnes (New York: Washington Square Press, Pocket Books, 1956), page 321. Hereafter designated in the text as BN.

12. Jean-Paul Sartre, *No Exit and Three Other Plays*, trans. Stuart Gilbert (New York: Vintage Books, 1955), p. 47.

13. Piotr Hoffman, *The Quest for Power – Hobbes, Descartes and the Emergence of Modernity* (New Jersey: Humanities Press, 1996).

14. "Power is everywhere; not because it embraces everything, but because it comes from everywhere." Michel Foucault, *The History of Sexuality*, vol. 1, *An Introduction* (New York: Vintage Books, Random House, 1980), p. 93.

15. Ibid., p. 94.

16. Ibid., vol. 2, *The Use of Pleasure* (New York: Vintage Books, Random House, 1986), p. 60.

17. Ibid., vol. 2, pp. 250f.

18. Ibid., vol. 2, p. 253.

19. Roger Scruton, *Sexual Desire – A Moral Philosophy of the Erotic* (New York: Free Press, Macmillan, 1986), p. 123.

20. Jean-Paul Sartre, *Existentialism* (New York: Philosophical Library, 1947), p. 45.

Chapter 7

℘

MUTUAL LOVE: ARISTOTLE AND LUCE IRIGARAY

When a man thinks of a true friend, he is looking at himself in the mirror.

—Cicero

We began with Plato's idea of erotic love, and finally we come around to consider his principal student and critic, Aristotle, and his idea of perfect friendship. Together, Plato and Aristotle are considered to be the fathers of Western philosophy, and they are often represented as having set the patterns for two contrasting mind-sets. The Platonists are held to be those who seek the ideal at the expense of the concrete and for whom the life of reason leads toward a vision of totality and perfection beyond particular and material things. Aristotelians, on the other hand, are represented as those who are more concerned with knowledge of actual things and whose reasoning is directed toward the realization of functional and practical goals rather than theoretical ideals.

Our purpose in considering Aristotle at this point is not so much to determine whether he contradicts or complements Plato, although these are not irrelevant considerations, but to see Aristotle's notion of mutual love as an alternative to Sartre's view of love as inevitable conflict. Obviously, since Aristotle wrote some twenty-three hundred years ago, his work cannot be considered a "response" in a literal historical sense. However, both Aristotle and Sartre would agree that human selfhood is inconceivable apart from one's relation to another person. Both argue that I require another in order to see — be — my self. The difference is that Sartre's "other" is inevitably threatening, while Aristotle's "other" is so much akin to me that he is like another self. Sartre's analysis results in endless reflections so labyrinthine that the substance of the self seems to be lost, while Aristotle's more down-to-earth approach suggests that love enhances and strengthens the self.

Aristotle's view is not without its problems, however. The historical context of his thinking is very remote from ours and very different. Classical Athens, where he spent much of his life, may have invented the world's first democracy, but political participation did not include the large slave population, women, or the many foreigners who lived in the city. Moreover, Aristotle was Macedonian by birth and his family had long-standing ties with the royal house there. Aristotle was himself a tutor to the young prince Alexander, soon to show himself to be a military genius who would seize leadership of all the Greek city-states in his dream of world empire.

We should not be surprised, therefore, to find that Aristotle's thinking about human relationships would be focused primarily on men who were actively involved in political and economic leadership. Indeed, he says that political activity aims at the highest and noblest of all human goods, and he compares this kind of competitive striving to the Olympic Games, where mere good looks and strength are not enough, but honor is won by those who join the contest and compete successfully. To act in the fullest sense, therefore, one must be fully engaged in the political arena. This is happiness, this is living well, says Aristotle, because one is making the most of all one's potentialities, and by this he means not only one's intellectual and physical abilities but also one's friends and social resources as well.[1] One could not achieve self-fulfillment in the largest sense without friends.

This ethic of self-realization, making the most of one's potential, is inherently elitist because we are not all equally endowed with intelligence, strength, ambition, or social position. Aristotle well understood this and simply took it for granted that the goal of excellence would only be achieved by a few. In his view, the world is basically hierarchical in its structure: everything exists in a higher

or lower relation to everything else. The essence of each thing, its
nature, moves it to fulfill its limited degree of potentiality to the
best of its ability. Human beings are different from the rest of nature
because we have the capacity to choose the means for the
actualization of our potential. This is what makes us moral
creatures: there are better and worse (or, right and wrong) ways
for us to pursue excellence. Our choice of friends is therefore quite
crucial, because in Aristotle's view they are necessary for the
achievement of excellence.

In order to further explore the idea of mutual love, and to bring
a critical perspective to bear on Aristotle's elitist and masculine
presumptions, I will also include the contemporary feminist voice
of Luce Irigaray, French psychoanalyst and philosopher. Irigaray
has come to increasing prominence ever since 1974 when her book,
Speculum of the Other Woman, presented a decisive critique of
Freudian-Lacanian theory because of its monopolistic focus on male
sexuality. In numerous books and articles Irigaray has attempted
to redefine women's psychology by making the female body the
standard of discourse.

Even though their starting points could hardly be more distant,
what strikes our attention is the way in which Irigaray's language
echoes Aristotle's on the most crucial point. "When you say I love
you, ..." says Irigaray, "you're saying I love myself."[2] Aristotle's
language is very similar: "In loving a friend men love what is
good for themselves" (*NE* 1157b34). In both cases, love of another
is inextricably linked to self-love because of the sameness of the
other. The full scope of what this means in Aristotle and Irigaray,
of course, diverges quite significantly, but nonetheless both seem
to be pointing to an ideal of perfect reciprocity in their definition
of love.

THE DEFINING RELATION

Since Aristotle's comments on this theme in the *Nicomachean
Ethics* as well as elsewhere are usually translated as "friendship,"
we have to ask whether he is talking about something other than
love. The problem is complicated in the classical Greek texts because
there are three different words in Greek — *eros, philia,* and *agape* —
that can be translated as "love." Whether or not clear distinctions
can be made in the meanings of these words has been the subject

of considerable ongoing debate among scholars, especially since some Christian theologians attempt to find a single meaning for the word *agape* that refers only to God's love.[3] Gregory Vlastos and other scholars point out that in Greek these words are not so distinct in their meaning. "*Philia* is a near synonym of *agape*," says Vlastos.[4] With regard to the question of "love" versus "friendship" in Aristotle's texts, I find Vlastos's argument persuasive that what Aristotle means by *philia* is not adequately rendered in English unless it is understood "as a special case of inter-personal love." "Love," says Vlastos, "is the only English word that is robust and versatile enough" to carry the force of what Aristotle means to say.[5]

In any case, since the working definition we assumed at the outset is that "love is finding oneself in another," Aristotle's discussion of friendship could hardly be more pertinent. Friendship is based on "a kind of likeness" (*NE* 1155a34), says Aristotle, in which there is a mutual recognition of "goodwill and wishing well to each other" (*NE* 1156a5). Mutuality is of the essence.

In order to set up his definition of perfect friendship, Aristotle first observes that there are two lesser forms of friendship based on utility and on pleasure. A friendship of utility may amount to little more than the normal cordiality that attends a commercial transaction—"service with a smile" so that your customers will come back—or, more important, two people may become friends because they are engaged in the same projects, and make helpful contacts for one another. The essential thing is their mutual usefulness, in which there is an exchange of benefits. The friendship would not long survive if it became one sided, if one were only a taker and never a giver.

Friendships of pleasure are similar to those of utility in their expectations of reciprocity. You cannot expect to be invited to your friends' parties if you are unpleasant to them, and you are expected to invite them to your parties if they invite you. The test of friends, to put it frankly, is whether or not they are fun. This kind of relationship is most typical of the young, says Aristotle, because they are so much more under the sway of their emotions and what is immediately before them. Such friendships change quickly because pleasures are so alterable.

Aristotle's hard-headed appraisal of most friendly relations may seem a little harsh, but one cannot deny its accuracy. The fact is, most of the people we call friends are either friends of utility or pleasure, preferably both. We do not sustain many friendships — probably not any — in which we perceive nothing advantageous to ourselves.

Aristotle follows Plato in assuming that pursuing one's self-interest is normal and natural. All men seek the good. Plato thought that the tendency of self-interest to become narrow and exclusive could be overcome by the abolition of private property and the family (*Republic* bks. 3 & 5). Aristotle, on the other hand, seems much more inclined to accept the conventions of family and community life as given and then seek by careful calculations of proportion and benefit to broaden the inclinations of self-interest.

The point of Aristotle's analysis is not to condemn such relationships; he is realistic enough to see that networks of exchange relationships are how the world works. His point is to move us from these transactional levels of mutuality toward a higher, more ideal kind of friendship — not unlike the way Diotima moves Socrates up the ladder of love in the *Symposium* — a much rarer kind of friendship in which men wish well to each other not for some incidental benefit but because "they are good in themselves." This is the true or "perfect friendship of men who are good, and alike in virtue" (*NE* 1156b6–9). Utility and pleasure are not precluded in this kind of friendship because goodness is both useful and pleasant. True friends do help each other and enjoy each other's company, but these are results of true friendship and not its basis.

True friendships are "based on a certain resemblance" of character (*NE* 1156b21) that is not simply a given, but is built up over a lifetime by the kinds of choices the partners make (*NE* 1157b31). This is no easy task, as Aristotle warns earlier: it requires the prudent application of rational principles to avoid either excess or deficiency toward the right people in just the right way at just the right times (*NE* 1106b–1107a). This is how virtuous men resemble each other, in the exercise of reasoned choices that make civic life possible. There is a reciprocity in this kind of friendship, but it is an exchange in which "each gets from each in all respects the same as, or something like what, he gives" (*NE* 1156b35). That is to say, in a true friendship there is no advantage to be gained or lost. A kind of disinterested parity exists in which each can genuinely wish the good of the other.

This is the defining relation: mutual love can only happen perfectly when the partners are so equal in virtue that each can wish the other well without suspicion or hope of advantage on either side. The key consideration is trust. Where there is inequality one can never be sure whether the attentions of the other are genuine or whether they are the contrivances of seduction or domination. Only in the absence of advantage, can "good men be friends for their own sake" and "friends without qualification" (*NE* 1157ab). While pursuing the good is a matter of self-interest, Aristotle recognizes that this cannot happen in an ideal way unless there is a constraining balance between the parties: "[O]nly good men can be friends: for bad men do not delight in each other unless some advantage come of the relation" (*NE* 1157a19). Good men can be friends because the good is one, unifying in its effects, while badness is disintegrating and alienating.

What holds the relationship together is merit. The two partners do not merely regard each other as individuals, but as bearers of a standard of quality or goodness that *both* strive for.

Aristotle by no means rules out the possibility of friendship between unequals—elder to younger, ruler to subject, husband to wife—in which each party neither gets the same from the other, nor seeks it. But the danger in an unequal relationship is exploitation, that one or both partners will use the relation to gain some personal advantage. To a young person, for example, an older person's greater knowledge, resources, and social connections are of obvious benefit. In return, the older person expects to receive honor and esteem from the younger person. Whether or not this is a relation of utility in the crass sense, it seems fairly obvious that there is some kind of exchange going on here. For either party to claim to love the other simply for "his own sake," apart from such expectations, seems naive.

In this kind of situation Aristotle believes that a kind of proper proportioning of love should take place to equalize the relation. Since the two do not meet as peers, the one of inferior status owes a greater amount of respect and affection to the one who is elder, ruler, or better in some way, than the latter does to him. The disproportion cannot be ignored. By acknowledging it the one who is inferior indicates a certain worthiness on his or her part to enter into the relationship. Without this recognition, even a disproportionate relationship would not be possible. Greater devotion thus somewhat compensates for lower status, argues Aristotle, "for when the love is in proportion to the merit of the parties, then in a sense arises equality, which is certainly held to be characteristic of friendship" (*NE* 1158b25).

The paradigm of mutual love is clearly equality. For Aristotle this seems to be the only way to prevent a loving relationship from degenerating into a manipulative power struggle of the kind Sartre describes so insightfully. It is important to remember that the parity that Aristotle calls for is not something static and identical to the two partners, but is the dynamic striving of two separate individuals to achieve excellence. Their goodness is thus "augmented by their companionship." True friends improve each other in the activity of their relationship, says Aristotle, "for from each other they take the mold of the characteristics they approve" (*NE* 1172a 12, 13). Like Sartre, Aristotle sees the importance of others in coming to know and to be our selves. We cannot see ourselves directly but only as we are reflected through the eyes of others. Where there is parity between lovers or friends, however, this reflection can be edifying instead of threatening.

Since Luce Irigaray also makes a case for love as a kind of perfect reciprocity, we have to first take into account her profound opposition to Aristotelian thinking. She has set herself dead against the conventional view accepted by Aristotle that women lack an essential nature in themselves and that they are dependent upon men for the realization of their potential.[6]

The whole point of her work is to show that virtually from the beginning of (patriarchal) Western culture women's nature has been construed to be a derivative or subsidiary form of masculine characteristics. There is no parity between the sexes. Because male sexuality is taken as the standard, for example, women are not even regarded as a sex because they "lack" a visible, single sex organ. Hence, women are "this sex which is not one" — the title of a book she first published in 1977. (Actually, the title is deliberately ambiguous; she also means that women's sexuality is much more diverse and multiple than men's — i.e., not "one.")

True mutuality between the sexes is thus impossible, argues Irigaray, because all of our habits and even language itself characterizes women primarily in the distorted image of masculine values. Modern feminism, even though it has had some limited economic and political successes, has been misconceived because it is predicated on the assumption that women should become equal to men. "Women merely 'equal' to men would be 'like them,' therefore not women" (*This Sex* 165f). "Why not equal to themselves?" asks Irigaray. Instead of neutralizing or obliterating the difference between the sexes, she argues, equality between men and women cannot be achieved until the values of female sexuality are restored. What is important is for women to realize the importance of issues that are specific to them.[7]

Women do not need to be mediated to each other via the masculine. "She has a relation to herself that has no need of that guarantee dividing and joining the one (male and female) and the other. ...She needs only to embrace herself. Women only need to embrace each other for their truth to have a place."[8] This has to happen, Irigaray argues, for a woman to recover her subjectivity. As long as she remains the object of men's desire, she is passive, the receiver of initiative from man as the sole subject. The only remnant of her subjectivity is her power of seduction. "In my opinion," she says, "if there is a fall, it is located in the reduction of the feminine to the passive, to the past tense and to the object of man's pleasure, in the identification of the woman with the beloved (*aimée*)" (*Reader* 185). What has to emerge is woman's self-love or she will continue to be perceived as a means to male self-realization (*Reader* 191).

Thus, while Luce Irigaray obviously rejects the Aristotelian assumptions of masculine primacy, it is noteworthy that she also seems to be arguing that genuine love requires a kind of parity between the participants, an argument that is not far from Aristotle's description of what takes place in a perfect friendship. Actually, Irigaray goes further because she rejects the whole exchange model that pervades Aristotle's discussion. Even in perfect friendship, it will be recalled, Aristotle speaks of how each partner gets from the other something like what he gives (*NE* 1156b35). Whereas Irigaray asserts that the exchange mentality is of masculine invention for masculine purposes. Love is not a transaction between sharply differentiated others who are enigmas to one another. "When you say I love you—staying right here, close to you, close to me—you're saying I love myself. You don't need to wait for it to be given back; neither do I. We don't owe each other anything. That 'I love you' is neither gift nor debt" (*This Sex* 206).

In fact, for Irigaray love is not really a "relation" at all; it is being so much "in touch" that there is no clear distinction between lover and beloved. The active-passive distinction is surpassed. It is not a matter of "one" or "two" in which the "you" and "I" are united, but a kind of undifferentiated presence that is physically communicated. "Are we alike?" she asks. "If you like. It's a little abstract. I don't quite understand 'alike.' Do you? Alike in whose eyes? In what terms? By what standard? With reference to what third? I'm touching you, that's quite enough to let me know that you are my body" (*This Sex* 208).

Thus, both Aristotle and Irigary point to an ideal of love that overcomes the inherent power struggle that arises when two separate individuals come together. Aristotle tries to do this by appealing to a notion of perfect parity in which the two partners are brought together by their mutual striving for excellence. Irigaray tries to counter this masculine standard of competitive striving by drawing attention to alternate feminine modes of commonalties and contiguities with themselves. For her, love is not the male problem of a parity of exchange, but an affirmation of feminine mutuality.

THE ROLE OF REASON

"All men by nature desire to know," says Aristotle in the first line of his *Metaphysics*, a statement that could equally well have been said by his mentor, Plato. Both saw that knowledge could not be acquired dispassionately. Both saw that the close relationship, if not identity, between love and reason had important social consequences—Plato in his *Republic*, Aristotle in his *Politics*. Where the two differ is in their understanding of the object of love. For Plato, as we have seen, love begins with the particular, but leads progressively to a "good" that transcends all particulars. For Aristotle, love also begins with the particular, but finds the "good" immanent in its nature, in what it is capable of becoming.

Everything in nature functions according to what kind of thing it is. Plants and animals alike seek light, water, and food, but each does so in its own way, as determined by its biological equipment: "Everything that depends on the action of nature is by nature as good as it can be" (*NE* 1099b23). Thus, what is "good" varies according to species. Each seeks as efficiently as possible to be the kind of thing that it is: fish swim, birds fly, rabbits run. Humankind alone has the capacity to choose the means for actualizing its potential. This is why "all men by nature seek to know" — because we do not move automatically in fulfillment of our natures. We have to *think* about our goals and *plan* how to achieve them and then make the right *choices* to put our plans into action. We desire to know precisely because we do not already know. Therefore, the excellence of a person depends first on correctly understanding one's nature and then on acting appropriately to make the best of one's potentialities.

Uppermost in understanding human nature is Aristotle's declaration that "man is by nature a political animal."[9] This is necessarily so, argues Aristotle, because an isolated individual would be incapable by himself of discussion and deliberation about ends and means. The power of speech, in other words, is the origin of reason and moral consciousness, and this is what distinguishes man from all other creatures: "It is a characteristic of man that he alone has any sense of good and evil, of just and unjust" (*Pol.* 1253a15). Simply put, human reason is a function of our social nature. Thus, to be fully human is to live in associations where moral discourse is carried on — family, friends, and community. "He who is unable to live in a society," Aristotle observes dryly, "or who has no need because he is sufficient for himself, must be either a beast or a god" (*Pol.* 1253a28).

To live the good life, therefore, is more than satisfying biological drives and material necessities. Living well means living together in families and political communities: "These are created by friendship, for the will to live together is friendship" (*Pol.* 1280b39). And the reason for this is not merely to have companionship, but "for the sake of noble actions" (*Pol.* 1281a2). That is, the desire for friendship is the desire to fulfill one's human potentialities in the highest and deepest sense — "for with friends men are more able both to think and to act" (*NE* 1155a16). Friends are thus like an extension of the self because shared talk and deliberation enlarge our capacity to understand problems, consider alternative views, debate courses of action — as well as provide support in carrying out specific plans of action. For Aristotle, this is the good life: "living together and sharing in discussion and thought" (*NE* 1170b11-12). Mutuality and rationality are very closely linked.

Interestingly enough, Luce Irigaray strongly echoes Aristotle on the importance of public discourse in making life fully human. "The values of life," she says, "are not silent values. For human beings, life takes place and unfolds through speech (*la parole*). In order to promote the values of life, you have to begin to speak" (*Reader* 51). Until recently, she argues, women had been restricted to the realm of domestic material concerns, and it is now time for them to share publicly what had been previously felt only privately and individually.

But even more important, she goes on, women must "renew the whole of language" (*le langage*) so that they do not inadvertently "turn completely into men" by taking on "discourses of mastery"— the deadening grid of rationality that is so alien to the mobility and constant changeableness of women's experience (*Reader* 51). In this, of course, Irigaray breaks very decisively with Aristotle, for whom the rules of logic are what make meaningful discourse possible. For him, and the Western tradition generally, the principles of identity and noncontradiction are what enable "like to know like"— the basis of science as well as mutual love. To Irigaray, however, this standard of the "one" is a formal abstraction employed in language to systematically repress or exclude the living diversity of female experience. "Woman does not obey the principle of self-identity, or of identity with any particular x. She identifies with every x, without identifying with it in any particular way."[10] "If we keep on speaking sameness, if we speak to each other as men have been doing for centuries, as we have been taught to speak, we'll miss each other, fail ourselves" (*This Sex* 205).

The entire system of discourse predicated on identity and difference has more to do with logical form than with the immediacy of bodily life. The masculine drive for coherence is achieved at the price of being cut off from desire, pain, joy, the body—"living values." Of course, Irigaray concedes sarcastically, "it is important to have access to a certain rationality so as to be able to, say, 'play chess' with men" (*Reader* 51), but this is something quite alien to women's own discourse, which is fluid rather than linear, rich with bodily metaphors rather than abstract categories, inclusive and allusive rather than exclusive and possessive.

So, yes, women must speak out, but not in the language of masculine domination and control. Women have to "come out of" men's language in order to become themselves (*This Sex* 205).

Language must be revolutionized to establish a new kind of equilibrium between what is already established in the world and a new flowering of openness: "unfenced encounters wherein those who risk most come on towards the other and depart anew. Without restraint" (*Reader* 214).

What is interesting about Irigaray's vision of the future is her description of it in the language of love. That is, like Aristotle (and Plato) she sees that love is the foundation of human community, but instead of an ideal relation of clearly differentiated peers, the language Irigaray uses describes the unguarded experience of first love, as it is felt prior to rational understanding: "openness barred by no consciousness...foreign to any reflection...before any evaluation...prior to any relationship...spilling into one another. Acceptance of an open sea that cannot be mastered, of a multiplicity irreducible to the one. No geometry, no accounts here" (*Reader* 215).

Actually, the key to Irigaray's vision of love is the same as Aristotle's: trust. This is at the heart of Aristotle's argument for the careful pairing of two virtuous men—a relation in which distrust is banished because they stand in such perfect parity with one another: "[I]t is among good men that trust and the feeling that 'he would never wrong me'...are found." (*NE* 1157a20-24). Irigaray's affirmation of the importance of trust is just as strong, but she quarrels with the system of rational discourse precisely in order to get out from under language that breeds distrust by dividing women according to values of production and exchange. She calls for a new language of intimacy among women: "You keep our selves to the extent that you share us. You find our selves to the extent that you trust us" (*This Sex* 206). What Irigaray wants is "free of domination—in itself or in the other...a flowering environment in which those who are free of all fear would be embraced" (*Reader* 215-216).

On the role of reason in mutual love, therefore, Aristotle and Luce Irigaray divide quite sharply. For Aristotle, perfect mutuality would not be possible apart from rational discourse: virtuous men come together in shared discussions of excellence. For Irigary, perfect mutuality is only possible when rationality is abandoned for a new language that affirms the way women's lives touch each other, in the giving and receiving of themselves (*Reader* 218).

THE ROLE OF SEXUALITY

In contrast to Plato, what is immediately apparent in Aristotle's discussion of mutual love is the absence of the element of sexual desire. For Plato, it will be recalled, sexual desire plays a powerful role in the initial levels of erotic love, but Aristotle is very restrained in what he has to say about the element of sexual attraction in friendship. Only in his consideration of the less than ideal forms of friendship, those of utility and pleasure, is there any suggestion that sexual satisfaction would be an aspect of the relationship, and even on this level it is not very prominent.

Since Aristotle otherwise seems so much more naturalistic in his thinking than Plato, we have to ask why this is so. The answer is that he has not ignored sexuality, but he has, on the one hand, demoted the sexual relation between men and women to a low level of significance, while, on the other hand, he has raised the relation between men *above* the sexual level.

Based on his studies of animal life, as well as his observations of human societies, Aristotle concludes that the relation between men and women is another example of the relation between *actuality* and *potentiality* that he has seen everywhere else in nature. Matter is virtually the same as raw potentiality, in Aristotle's view, because it can be made into almost anything by acting upon it with some plan or purpose. The stones in a riverbed, for example, could be made into a dam, or a roadway, or a fence, or a house, or even serve as missiles in warfare. Form actualizes potentiality. The form inherent in every living thing is its nature, its "essence," and is what determines the kind of thing it can be—acorns are potential oak trees, eggs are potential chickens. In the human sexual relation, to put it simply, man provides the "form" to woman's "matter" for the production of another human being. It is the (active) male essence that brings the (passive) female potentiality to fulfillment.

Given this disproportion between the sexes, Aristotle recognizes that between husband and wife a kind of "natural friendship" exists, not only for reproduction but also to help each other in performing their different functions (*NE* 1162a15). Both utility and pleasure are found in such friendships, but also virtue—"if the parties are good," that is, if both are performing their proper functions (*NE* 1162a27).

But it is clear that equality, the precondition for perfect friendship, is not possible between the sexes. "The male is by nature superior, and the female inferior; and the one rules, and the other is ruled" (*Pol.* 1254b14). This is not only true of humankind but is a general principle of nature: the soul over the body, the mind over passion, intellect over appetite, men over animals, parent over child, freemen over slaves. In all of these relations the rule is rational—that is, according to a principle that leads to the highest degree of fulfillment of which each is capable. In the case of woman, this does not mean that she lacks rational ability, but that she has it to the degree that it leads her to obedience (*Pol.* 1260a25).

For Aristotle, therefore, mutual love between man and woman in the highest sense is simply not possible. The gender gap is unsurpassable because there is no way for women to stand on a par with men. The sexual relationship of husband and wife may be a kind of friendship, yes, but it is of a distinctly lower order than what is possible between men. It is essentially a relation of *(re)production*, while between men who are equals friendship is a relation of *action*.[11]

A comparison between Plato and Aristotle is instructive on this point. Bodily functions are relatively unimportant to Plato because for him the distinctively human faculty is reason. Since Plato perceives that women are just as capable of intellectual activity as men (in the *Republic*, at least), he sees no justification for excluding them from the ruling elite (bk. 5, 454–455). The sexual distinction between "those who bear" and "those who beget" seems trivial by this rationalistic standard. Aristotle, in contrast, because of his common-sense, biological approach, takes differences in physical functions much more seriously, but relegates the child-bearing function to a lower order of significance than the realm of political action. If reproduction is the essential female function, then deliberation about the ends and means of life is the essential male function.

Luce Irigaray, as we have seen, rejects Plato's rationalism because of its abstract formalism, its indifference to the lived experience of women. In her view this would amount to conceiving of women in terms of male discourse. Equality on these terms would represent a loss instead of a gain. And, of course, she rejects Aristotle's identification of women's nature (her essence) with her reproductive function.

In her own way, however, Irigaray appears to follow the biologism of Aristotle's approach. Bodies, both male and female, are central to her thinking. But her difference from Aristotle could not be greater: Irigaray's interest is in what the body *represents*, its social significance, not in its literal biological nature. The whole thrust of her work is to break apart the assumption that bodies, male or female, are identical with their meaning. Her criticism of Aristotle (and all patriarchal discourse) is not an attack on male sexuality as such, but on its establishment in language and culture as the definitive model of what it means to be human. Anatomy is not the crucial issue, in other words, but the meanings and values that are ascribed *to* anatomy.

What Irigaray attempts to do, therefore, is, first, deny the primacy of the male paradigm as the sole standard for understanding sexuality; and, second, shift the focus of female sexual identity from reproduction to self-satisfaction (*jouissance*). A woman does not need to be a mother in order to be woman. What makes a woman a woman is not her reproductive capacity (for which she needs a man), but her capacity to have pleasure in and with herself (for which she does not need a man).

In Irigaray's new paradigm, love is not defined as love of another sex, which is inherently divisive (between one kind and another kind) and carries an inevitable transactional connotation. For her, love begins in female autoeroticism, with the self-touching that emerges from the multiplicity of woman's erogenous possibilities. The very nature of her sex organs keeps her "constantly in touch" with herself. "Woman has sex organs more or less everywhere," Irigaray emphasizes. "She finds pleasure almost anywhere." This is what characterizes her sexuality, not the reproductive function. Only from a male point of view is her sexuality identified essentially in terms of the single function of reproduction. Neither the vagina (as a receptacle for the penis) nor the clitoris (as an analog to the penis) defines female sexuality. It is *both* and *more*. Irigaray seizes upon the metaphor of the "two lips" as an image by which to emphasize the polymorphic nature of female sexuality. In herself, she is plural, not "one," nor does she need an "other" in the conventional sense. "'She' is indefinitely other in herself" (*This Sex* 26, 28f).[12]

From autoeroticism Irigaray extends her concept of love to homosexuality. Thus, love in the ideal sense would be of an other who is so much like me that there is no sense of estrangement to be overcome. "I love you: body shared, undivided. Neither you nor I severed." For Irigaray, one does not find oneself in the other; in some sense one *is* the other. "Neither one nor two," she says, "I've never known how to count" (*This Sex* 206, 207). This felt identity seems very similar to what was expressed by Irigaray's philosophical predecessor, Simone de Beauvoir, in her characterization of love between women as a "mirroring" relation, one that dissolves the distinction between self and other, in contrast to the transactional love between men and women that re-enforces the distinction.[13] Love understood as this mutuality of intimacy is very immediate and sensual, innocent of all cultural and institutional regulation. Irigaray asks, "What need have I for husband or wife, for family, persona, role, function? Let's leave all those to men's reproductive laws. I love you, your body, here and now. I/you touch you/me, that's quite enough for us to feel alive" (*This Sex* 209).

The outcome, then, of our examination of both Aristotle's and Irigaray's thinking about love is that neither one seems to think that the gender gap can be overcome. In both cases, differences of sexual identity preclude the ideal of mutual love. In both cases, true mutuality can only be achieved by minimizing differences and focusing on the likeness or sameness of the partners to each other. Aristotle says that a true friend is "like another self" (*NE* 1170b7), and Irigary goes even further when she speaks of how love makes "You/I" inseparable (*This Sex* 209). For where there is a substantive difference, there emerges the possibility of maneuver for advantage. Where this possibility exists, there is uncertainty and distrust— and perfect love vanishes. As both Aristotle and Irigaray demonstrate, the logic of mutual love leads almost inexorably to same-sex love.

OUTCOMES

Is the idea of mutual love strong enough to overcome the ambiguity that inevitably enters a relationship in which two self-identities struggle for recognition?

The answer I would propose is that Aristotle's concept of perfect friendship comes close to successfully dealing with the problem, although its formulation must be so narrow that it will be beyond the reach of satisfying many who would espouse such an ideal.

As we saw in his preliminary discussion of friendships of utility and pleasure, Aristotle is a tough-minded realist about human relationships. He begins by taking account of the calculations of self-interest that enter into interpersonal associations. That is, he takes the struggle for power as a given but then seeks to neutralize this factor by defining friendship in such a way that the partners stand in balance with each other. If neither partner has an advantage over the other, each can wish the other well for his own sake. The competitive striving is never entirely eliminated, but actually unites them because they are striving for excellence: "from each other they take the mold of the characteristics they approve" (*NE* 1172a14). Behind Aristotle's idea of virtue is the Homeric drive to be the best, to act in such a way that the nobility of one's deeds and character never fade from human esteem.[14]

The equality between two men that is necessary for true friendship is not specified in quantitative terms by Aristotle. The striving for excellence is a matter of being all that you can be—fulfilling one's potentialities. In principle, at least, two people who are very unlike each other in important respects could be alike in the degree to which they make the most of their natural endowments. In principle, it would seem that they could be friends or lovers. Always the realist, however, it is clear that Aristotle does not think that this is likely. The fact is that happiness and self-fulfillment require certain external goods. "For it is impossible, or not easy, to do noble acts without the proper equipment," he says, and frankly includes in this category such things as friends, riches, political power, good birth, good children, and good looks (*NE* 1099b1–8). In practice, then, because such things enhance one's capacity for action, the perfection of friendship requires comparable assets and status of both partners.

It is apparent, then, that external goods and quantitative considerations such as age play an important part in the determination of virtue and perfect friendship. Obviously, such a relationship will be exceedingly rare since the possibility of finding another who is my equal in so many respects (socially, economically, intellectually, etc.) reduces the prospects considerably. But Aristotle goes even further and argues that friendship in the deepest sense is really a shared life that "requires time and familiarity" in order for love and trust to develop (*NE* 1156b25). "There is nothing so characteristic of friends as living together" (*NE* 1157b19), he says, holding property in common and taking pleasure in common pursuits, "for friendship depends on community" (*NE* 1159b33).

The full scope of Aristotle's idea, therefore, has both sociological depth and temporal continuity. It is not just the happy coincidence of temperament and like-mindedness. The equality essential to mutual love necessarily extends to very concrete and material considerations that both limit it as an ideal but also greatly strengthen its stability.

Aristotle may not have read Hobbes and Sartre, but it is clear that in working out his ideal of perfect friendship, he has carefully taken into account many of the factors that throw a relationship into disequilibrium—age, wealth, status, gender. He knows that unequal powers are likely to lead to exploitation and resentment. His realistic acknowledgment of their importance is what leads him to insist on equality as the essential element in mutual love. "Perfect friendship is the friendship of men who are good, and alike in virtue" (*NE* 1156b7), he says repeatedly, but he makes it clear that the good is relative to the parties involved in all kinds of material, quantitative ways. A friendship of perfect reciprocity may be impossibly ideal, but Aristotle has shown that it can be approached by a judicious and candid regard for a balance of powers in the relationship. This may be as good a case for mutual love as can be made.

How does Luce Irigaray's view of mutual love look in response to the question of power? Instead of attempting to establish an equilibrium, Irigaray seeks to dismantle the masculine structures of discourse that, in her view, instigate alienation, resentment, and distrust. Without the artificiality and formality of traditional rationality, Irigaray envisions a kind of pre-critical intimacy among women that is prior to the question of identity and difference, thus obviating the power problem altogether.

Irigaray's claim that there are more direct and intuitive ways of knowing, more closely related to actual lived experience than traditional rational discourse, is not such a radical departure if one thinks of the work of Henri Bergson, for example. And the possibility of different kinds of discourse, with a multiplicity of "logics," or conventions of meaning, has been anticipated in the later work of Ludwig Wittgenstein. What *is* new is the daring way Irigaray both embraces Nietzsche in his deconstructive assault on fixed forms of being and also turns the tables on him with her lyrical reconception of lived experience in fluid and feminine terms rather than combative and masculine language. She becomes Nietzsche's ironical "marine lover."[15]

Whether Irigaray's rejection of rational discourse as inherently "phallocratic" adequately comes to grips with the power problem is another question. It seems overly simple to claim that the shifting dynamics between people who are in intimate and meaningful association are the result of the formalities of Aristotelian logic. The problem seems to have more to do with the development of consciousness and self-identity, as we saw in Hegel's Master-Slave parable. Irigaray's attempt to circumvent the evolution of the awareness of a separate (and threatening) "other" by generating a new kind of female body language does not seem to focus on the real issue. The struggle to be seen and heard, to be recognized and accepted, is going to happen in some form or other, regardless of gender, regardless of language. If anything, Irigaray's attack on rationality could make the problem worse because there is then no court of appeal in the face of arbitrary assertions of power.

Marcia Homiak argues further on this point, asserting that Aristotle's notion of a friend as "'another oneself' [NE 1166a32], meaning that they value and enjoy about each other what they value and enjoy about themselves," is a model women might very well take for themselves in order to avoid relations of unhealthy dependence. Love, in this sense, is not living through the lives of others, but taking pleasure in and sharing the rational activities of others whose lives may be very different from one's own. Self-esteem is not dependent upon the esteem of others. "Each is independent in the sense that each enjoys the activities in her individual life-plan as well as the higher-level activities her plan shares with the plans of her friends."[16]

The final outcome we have to consider is whether the logic of mutual love leads inexorably to same-sex love (that is, does it rule out the possibility of heterosexual love?) as both Aristotle and Irigaray seem to imply.

In the case of Aristotle, this conclusion seems hard to avoid, even though the bond between friends is one of merit—and not a matter of physical relations. Nonetheless, Aristotle takes sex seriously and for him the fundamental difference in natural functions leads necessarily to fulfillment of different kinds of excellence. Even if one could overlook his prejudice that the male is superior and the female inferior, one could still not say that men and women are equal. They are functionally different and the difference is significant. (Interestingly, Irigaray agrees with this and has dedicated her work to defining this difference, but in non-Aristotelian terms.) This does not mean that Aristotle is an advocate of homosexual practices. (He explicitly disapproves of this as "brutish" [*NE* 1148b27–30].) What it does mean is that a sexual relation, say, between husband and wife, would necessarily be of a lower order of importance than a friendship between men who were peers. If love is a matter of finding oneself in another, then in Aristotle's view the other must be one who is like me in gender so as to make possible the most nearly perfect kind of reciprocity.

The only way around this is to argue that the sexual difference is not important, as Plato does, and that what matters is a meeting of the minds, because that *is* what is important. Or, conceivably, one might argue that a man and a woman might become friends at the point in their lives when sex is no longer important — that is, true mutuality might be achievable when the fulfillment of their sexual functions is no longer their essential characteristic. For many couples this may very well be what takes place in a later stage of their lives. For others, the sense of partnership and mutuality may prevail from the outset precisely because the sexual function is already relegated to a lower order of importance. Where sexuality is of primary importance, however, we have learned from both Aristotle and Luce Irigaray that mutual love will be problematic, at best.

In Irigaray's case, however, there are suggestions that her affirmation of same-sex love may not be her full intent. In several instances her argument seems to be that love between women is a first step to establishing their own separate consciousness of themselves as a sex. Women need to become aware of themselves as a gender apart from any reference to the male sex or the reproductive role they play in relation to men. This is the reason for her stress on woman's capacity for sexual self-satisfaction, that is, to establish female sexuality on its own terms and not as a means for fulfillment of male sexuality. What Irigaray seems to be aiming at is not simply a justification of female homosexuality, but of woman's sexual autonomy.

If this can be accomplished, Irigaray points toward a wholly new relation between the sexes in which men would meet women as something genuinely different from themselves and not as their derivative or possession. The appropriate passion for this encounter, she speculates, would be "wonder." Why wonder? Because the experience of wonder is more a beholding from a separate space than a merging in one space. Wonder takes place when one "sees something always for the first time, and never seizes the other as its object. Wonder cannot seize, possess or subdue such an object. The latter, perhaps, remains subjective and free?" (*Reader* 172). Irigaray rejects the idea of love in which one either consumes the other or is consumed by the other. In her ideal of love each allows the other to grow freely: "For such love to exist, each one must keep its body autonomous. One must not be the source of the other, nor the other or the one. Two lives must embrace and fecundate each other with no preconceived goal or end for the other."[17] For Irigaray, then, the mutuality of homosexuality might be better understood as a step in the evolution of genuine heterosexual mutuality where each sex could see the other as authentically *other*, and not as a reflection or projection of masculine values.

Here is a vision of mutual love, then, that ultimately turns out to be heterosexual, but is based on a drastic reconception of what sexuality might be — a sexuality grounded in one's own self-sufficiency and one that fully accepts the autonomy and equality of the other. Where this is the case, as Irigaray suggests, there may be no clear distinction between love of oneself and love of the other.

ASSESSMENT

What can we expect of mutual love?

Mutuality — togetherness, companionship — is typically assumed to be something that naturally accompanies love, one of its pleasant by-products. "My lover is my best friend," some people say. But we see from our examination of the preceding concepts of love that this may be easier said than done. Indeed, these other ideas of love seem to preclude the stability and balanced parity that is uppermost in mutual love. Erotic love pursues what it does not have; Christian love depends on a transcendent other; romantic love's craving for intensity would not be satisfied with mere mutuality; and love's conflicted struggle for recognition, as Sartre shows us, inherently undermines any notion of mutual trust. Only moral love, especially Kant's high regard for the autonomy of persons, comes close to approximating the ideal of mutuality. Here, however, it is apparent that the premium on personal integrity ultimately outweighs the kind of sharing and reciprocity that Aristotle and Irigaray talk about.

So mutual love is very much a distinct idea and must be understood on its own terms. Its key principle is equality, which is necessary in order to establish a relationship in which neither fear nor desire play a role. If there is no advantage to be gained or lost, each can genuinely wish the good for the other and expect the good from the other.

Is this realistic? Is it even remotely possible for two people to be on such an even par with each other not only materially but also socially, emotionally, and intellectually that neither has an edge on the other? Probably not. There is a tradition, quoted by Jacques Derrida,[18] that Aristotle himself often repeated, "O my friends, there is no friend."[19] That is, given Aristotle's criteria for perfect friendship, there could be no actual instance of it. It is an impossible ideal, an empty concept. Perhaps one could read this exclamation as a cry of despair, but, if so, why devote two whole books to the subject—books 8 and 9 of his *Nicomachean Ethics* —as well as key statements in his *Politics*? More likely, I think, Aristotle meant us to understand that mutual love is a goal, a human potentiality that may never be fully actualized but which nevertheless defines us as human beings.

No human potentiality is perfectly and fully realizable. We are always capable of change, we can always improve, we can always do better. So it is with mutual love. The fact that we do not do it perfectly does not mean it is not worth doing. It is achievable to the degree that attention is paid to balanced status, equal regard, comparable merit. The greater the degree of parity between the partners, the greater the possibility of genuine reciprocity. Both Aristotle and Luce Irigaray show us the possibility of mutual love, but they also show us that it is only realizable by means of tough-minded grappling with political realities and can only be actualized by very concrete considerations that build up loving friends in equal measure to each other. Good intentions and good feeling are not enough. Where real parity is missing, the greater the possibility for distrust and the breakdown of mutuality.

Mutual love is like other human potentialities—athletic, artistic, intellectual, political—none of which is ever fulfilled perfectly and finally, but striving to perform them as excellently as possible is what constitutes happiness.

FURTHER READING

The primary sources for Aristotle's concept of mutual love are his *Nicomachean Ethics* and his *Politics*. Both of these treatises are readily available in a variety of translations and both can be found in Richard McKeon's *Introduction to Aristotle*, 2d ed., rev. and enl. (Chicago: University of Chicago Press, 1973).

A brief overview of Aristotle's thinking is presented in a very readable book by Timothy A. Robinson: *Aristotle in Outline* (Indianapolis: Hackett Publishing Co., 1995).

Michel Foucault's *The Use of Pleasure*, vol. 2 of *History of Sexuality* (New York: Vintage Books, Random House, 1986), includes Aristotle in his social analysis of ancient Greek sexual morality.

Two fine scholarly studies on Aristotle are A. W. Price, *Love and Friendship in Plato and Aristotle* (Oxford: Clarendon Press, 1989) and Suzanne Stern-Gillet, *Aristotle's Philosophy of Friendship* (Albany: State University of New York Press, 1995).

Luce Irigaray's first book, *Speculum of the Other Woman*, trans. Gillian C. Gill (Ithaca: Cornell University Press, 1974), is intellectually challenging because so much of her argument about female sexuality is involved with an extensive critique of the psychoanalytic theories of Jacques Lacan. She continues her reconsideration of the status of women in the somewhat more accessible *This Sex Which Is Not One*, trans. Catherine Porter with Carolyn Burke (Ithaca: Cornell University Press, 1985).

The Irigaray Reader, ed. Margaret Whitford (Cambridge, Mass.: Basil Blackwell, 1991), is the best single-volume introduction to Irigaray's thinking.

Revaluing French Feminism, ed. Nancy Fraser and Sandra Lee Bartky (Bloomington: Indiana University Press, 1992), has three essays of significance to readers of chapter two and chapter seven of this book:

Luce Irigaray, "Sorcer Love: A Reading of Plato's *Symposium*, Diotima's Speech," pp. 60–76

Andrea Nye, "The Hidden Host: Irigaray and Diotima at Plato's *Symposium*," pp. 77–93

Diana J. Fuss, "'Essentially Speaking': Luce Irigaray's Language of Essence," pp. 94–112

NOTES

1. Aristotle, *Nicomachean Ethics*, 1099a5, 1099b. All quotations are from *Introduction to Aristotle,* trans. and ed. Richard McKeon, 2d ed., rev. and enl. (Chicago: University of Chicago Press, 1973). Hereafter designated in the text as *NE.*

2. Luce Irigaray, *This Sex Which Is Not One*, trans. Catherine Porter (Ithaca, N.Y.: Cornell University Press, 1985), p.206.

3. See chapter 3, note 12.

4. Gregory Vlastos, *Platonic Studies* (Princeton: Princeton University Press, 1973, 1981), p. 6 n. 13.

5. Ibid., p. 4.

6. Luce Irigaray, *Speculum of the Other Woman* (Ithaca, N.Y.: Cornell University Press, 1985), pp. 160–167.

7. Luce Irigaray, *The Irigaray Reader,* ed. Margaret Whitford (Cambridge, Mass.: Basil Blackwell, 1991), pp. 32f.

8. Luce Irigaray, *Marine Lover of Friedrich Nietzsche,* trans. Gillian C. Gill (New York: Columbia University Press, 1991), p. 85.

9. Aristotle, *Politics,* 1253a. All quotations are from *Introduction to Aristotle,* trans. and ed. Richard McKeon, 2d ed. rev. and enl. (Chicago: University of Chicago Press, 1973). Hereafter designated in the text as *Pol.*

10. Irigaray, *The Irigaray Reader,* p. 56; see also idem, *Marine Lover,* pp. 86–88.

11. Hannah Arendt's distinction between the life of action as opposed to labor and work is indispensable here. See her *The Human Condition* (Chicago: University of Chicago Press, 1958), pp. 7–13, and chapters 2 and 5.

12. For understanding of this point I am indebted to Elizabeth Grosz and have adopted some of her language in my discussion. See her *Sexual Subversions* (Boston: Allen & Unwin, 1989), pp. 110–117.

13. Simone de Beauvoir's argument seems explicitly designed as a reply to *her* mentor, Jean-Paul Sartre: "Between women love is contemplative; caresses are intended less to gain possession of the other than gradually to re-create the self through her; separateness is abolished, there is no struggle, no victory, no defeat; in exact reciprocity each is at once subject and object, sovereign and slave; duality becomes mutuality." *The Second Sex,* trans. H. M. Parshley (New York: Bantam Books, 1961), p. 391.

14. See the friendship of Glaukos and Diomedes in the *Iliad,* VI. 145–231.

15. Irigaray, *Marine Lover of Friedrich Nietzsche.*

16. Marcia L. Homiak, "Feminism and Aristotle's Rational Ideal," in *A Mind of One's Own – Feminist Essays on Reason and Objectivity*, ed. Louis M. Antony and Charlotte Witt (Boulder: Westview Press), p. 13.

17. Luce Irigaray, *Passions élémentaires* (1982) 32–33, quoted in *Sexual Subversions*, p. 170. See also Luce Irigaray, *An Ethics of Sexual Difference*, trans. Carolyn Burke and Gillian C. Gill (Ithaca, N.Y.: Cornell University Press, 1995), especially the chapter on Descartes's "Passions of the Soul."

18. Jacques Derrida, "The Politics of Friendship," *The Journal of Philosophy* 85 (1988): 632–644.

19. Immanuel Kant attributes the statement to Socrates. See his *Lectures on Ethics*, trans. Louis Infield (New York: Harper Torchbooks, 1963), p. 202.

Chapter 8

ℰↄ

CONCLUSION

Love, but take heed what you love.

—St. Augustine

In the introduction I suggested that much of our confusion about love had to do with the way we think about it. As we have seen in these six ideas, most of our thinking about love seems to be an attempt to solve the problem of loneliness. Even though we also deal with our solitude in other ways, through work and political life and other kinds of socializing, love seems more important because it is more all-encompassing and is closer to our sense of identity. For that reason we expect a lot from love. It promises total meaning in return for total devotion. Half-hearted lovers need not apply.

The totality of love, however, is always defined in some specific way, in terms of certain assumptions and definitions. Love may be global in its reach, but we are specific in how we think about it. As a result, the problem is usually not that love fails to deliver, but that the meaning it delivers is a consequence of the particular way in which we define it. These six ideas of love are all rather totalitarian in their scope, and each carries within it an inexorable logic that anticipates its outcome and virtually precludes other ways of loving. In a not-so-funny way, we are all prisoners of love.

The virtue of all this is the meaning it provides. Despite all the vague generalities, we have something rather specific in mind when we think seriously about love. Getting clear about definitions and priorities establishes coherence and enables us to reflect on our experience and see where the logic of a particular way of loving leads.

As important as coherence is, however, it is not the only thing that makes an idea viable. There is also the degree to which it seems to reflect the facts of the situation. The focus of this book has been to examine the core structure of each idea of love. The question remains as to how adequately these ideas do in fact correspond to our experience.

In the final analysis this has to be a kind of empirical question — that is, it can only be answered by taking a hard look at our own lived experience to see if there is in fact an affirmative answer. This cannot be settled by producing evidence in the usual sense of the word — case studies, statistics, and the like. In the end, it is individual judgment that determines whether these six ideas, or any one of them, ring true. Not the quantity of data in support of them but the insight they bring will be ultimately decisive, and only the reader can be the final judge of that.

With this in mind, let us review the six ideas to consider what kinds of questions remain open to further reflection.

Plato showed us that if love is desire for what we lack, then it will be forever unsatisfied because we will discover little by little the enormity of what we lack. Sexual interest is simply the first appearance of a more profound desire to breach the walls of loneliness. Each gratified desire reveals a new desire that reaches further — *qualitatively* further. The difference between the excellence we seek and the partiality of the satisfactions we obtain means that erotic love is forever yearning.

But the hard question to this very high-minded view is whether sexual desire is actually the lowest manifestation of essentially a spiritual desire or whether these are really *two* different kinds of desire that cannot be reconciled with each other. Or even more seriously, is the situation perhaps the reverse of the way Plato saw it? Are the so-called higher forms of love merely sublimated (socialized) forms of what is essentially biological instinct? The key question each person would have to ask is whether erotic love really does contain within itself a discriminating factor that, if properly tutored, would lead it toward what is best and most beautiful.

In contrast to erotic love's pursuit of self-interest, the whole tendency of Christian love points us in a different direction. The relation to transcendence disengages the self from its network of natural necessities so that in the conventional sense it becomes "selfless" because it has no interests to promote or defend. By giving up my natural self, I get back my free self. I can be myself without fear or desire, and help to open up a space in which others can be themselves. The presence of transcendence (the Kingdom of God) obliterates the walls that Plato tried to overcome with erotic reason.

Regardless of our attitude about religion, there is something very compelling about this radical image of self-giving as the epitome of love. One can hardly argue with it. No justification seems necessary; nor, for that matter, would any be adequate. As countless Christian witnesses have demonstrated through the centuries—from the martyrdom of St. Stephen to Martin Luther King, Jr.—there is enormous power in selflessness. But there are questions that linger, nonetheless. If I am entirely without fear or desire, what does my self consist of? My relationship to God is what defines my self and establishes my absolute uniqueness, but what does this mean if it is "beyond" everything? Even more disturbingly, does Christian love really care about others? If every relation to another is mediated by the God-relation, this calls me to responsibility in some ways but ultimately separates me from others. They (and I) are in God's hands, as it were. Is it possible that ordinary human fellow-feeling, parochial and possessive as it is, might actually be more altruistic than Christian love?

Romantic love, as we saw, is closely related to Christian love, and like Christian love, is not at home in the ordinary world. The devotion given by the lover to the beloved is absolute and this lifts the relation quite out of worldly restraints. Romantic love thrives on "otherness." But instead of looking beyond themselves, romantic lovers look only at each other. This is its magic and this is its downfall. If it comes to earth there is bound to be colossal disappointment, because the lovers turn out to be human, after all, and if it does not come to earth there is bound to be suffering, because the world will not indulge their freedom.

Or will it? The key to romantic love is freedom. Its defiance of every practical and moral constraint is what makes it so exhilarating and would seem to doom any attempt at domestication. If the other "owes" me affection, in other words, how can I be sure that it is freely given? But this is the question that has to be asked: Does the establishment of a fixed relation between lover and beloved, say in marriage, automatically preclude the kind of freedom requisite for romantic intensity? The reply to this might be that the existence of a formal bond still leaves open the disposition of the individual spirit within that context—which can be freely given or withheld. If love is the gift of freedom, in other words, is it necessarily compromised by a fixed relationship?

The answer of moral love is to reject this antithesis. Freedom and fidelity are not contraries. The lover's gift to the beloved is the gift of constancy, of absolute fidelity. The task is to convert unaccountable and unpredictable freedom into something concrete, something understandable, something reliable. To do this requires defining self-giving in an almost contradictory way so that it is in my self-interest to maintain it. Kant does this by subordinating the self to rational principles; Kierkegaard does this by identifying the self with its choices. The freedom of the self is thus transmuted into the consistency and integrity that moral love calls for.

The question that must be answered, however, is whether this actually amounts to a major change in idea. Is the unconditional gift of the self the same thing as a guarantee of the self's integrity? Is this a shift from finding oneself in another human being with godlike freedom to finding oneself in a rational principle or in a consistent pattern of behavior? Can the focus on the individuality of the beloved be maintained if the consistent logic of the relation is what is uppermost?

The questions about moral love, regardless of how we answer them, enable us to see how single-minded this view is. Variations of circumstance or the opinions of others are all exterior factors that cannot be allowed a decisive role without undercutting the lover's integrity. But can anyone live so walled up in his own moral castle? Jean-Paul Sartre showed us that such a view was not only unrealistic, but impossible. Because we cannot witness our own actions, we are inevitably dependent on those who do, he argues. There is an inescapable reciprocity in the human situation. My sense of self, the significance of my actions, requires the recognition of others. To love is both to confer the power of reflection on another and at the same time to try to control that reflection. We *must* find ourselves in others — although at the same time we must also overcome their regard in order not to be in bad faith. In the last analysis we cannot pretend that anyone other than ourselves is responsible for our character.

But can individual autonomy be asserted so simply and confidently? If love is a power struggle between two centers of freedom, then the question is whether there is any independent option. Is there such a thing as "good faith"? If my only choices involve the manipulation of another's freedom, what would sincerity or authenticity mean? Can I in fact have a sense of my self that is genuinely my own and not a reflection of someone else's?

Aristotle and Luce Irigaray also hold the view that reciprocal relations are central to human life, but they disagree with Sartre's contention that these can only be relations of conquest or submission. Neither denies the power dimension in human affairs. The whole point of Irigaray's work, in fact, is to drastically alter the traditional power structure between men and women that she, at least partly, lays at Aristotle's door. But both Aristotle and Irigaray maintain that reciprocity can be edifying rather than menacing. Mutual love is possible by building up a realistic equilibrium between the loving partners. Within this context what each partner finds in the other is a shared desire for the good rather than a threat to their very being.

The prevailing assumption throughout this view of mutual love, especially in Aristotle's case, is that material and qualitative differences cannot be ignored. To put it simply, *like loves like*, and mutual love is only possible on this premise. But is it true that significant differences in status inevitably turn love into a power relation between advantaged and disadvantaged? How much parity has to be established to neutralize the power struggle? Is there any realistic possibility for establishing mutuality on some basis that transcends the limiting hard facts of social and economic life?

Most disquieting of all is the skepticism that both Aristotle and Irigaray show about the possibility of genuine mutuality between men and women. Sex may be necessary, but mutual love is quite another matter. Disparity of biological and social functions and disparity even in cultural symbols and language usage would seem to imply that the gender wars will be ongoing. Or is it possible that a sea change in attitudes is under way? Might the concrete advances in political and economic equality for women foreshadow the establishment of a new parity between the sexes?

Finally, we have to ask, are we in fact captive to one or the other of these ideas of love? Are we prisoners of the logic of our own intentions? On the one hand we see how powerful each of these ideas is in providing meaning to our experience. "The defining relation" in each case sets priorities in motion that require a certain consistency. When we think about love in this way, we are in no doubt as to what it means, although we may not always be happy with it. The ecstatic meaning of romantic love, for example, is more likely to entail profound suffering than happiness. In other cases the full reach of meaning may be oddly contrary to what we expect. The pursuit of self-interest in erotic love, for example, moves toward almost selfless identification with qualities of beauty and excellence. Moral love, in its preoccupation with integrity, seems to lose touch with the one who inspired the commitment to fidelity in the first place. And the logic of mutual love, as we have just noted, turns out to require a degree of likeness between the partners that borders on exclusivity. Ironies seem to abound when we try to think seriously about love.

Despite the power of these ideas to clarify our experience, however, they are not the same as experience. As we all know, the actual experience of love is rarely so well defined. Even if we do think clearly, we rarely behave accordingly. In real life love is full of promise and does not pay close attention to limit and consistency and ironical possibilities. With enough dreaming and daring there is nothing to keep us from embracing intentions that are incompatible or even potentially disastrous. Life itself seems to entice us to do this. The price we pay, of course, is suffering. Real pain and conflict erupt when the contradictory aims of different ideas of love make their claims upon us, and only the strongest hearts can endure.

We know, too, that how we care and how we feel about others does not remain constant. Even if I hold to a consistent attitude, which is unlikely, what is to keep the other to the same view? Nothing can compel us to love, nor keep us from loving. Since so much of love has to do with freedom, there is a fluid, constantly moving quality about it. One cannot step twice in the same river,

Heraclitus said. This may be especially true of love: change is its only reality.

Further, in the real experience of love there are nearly always extraneous factors that complicate the dynamics of our most meaningful relationships. Work and career responsibilities, for instance, often demand as much, or more, of our time and attention than our relations to those who ostensibly matter most to us. Distinguishing between love and work may be fairly easy for some people, but for others, especially professional persons, the love of their work may in fact be the most important relationship in which they find themselves. If this is the case, then the six ideas examined here might also be useful in analyzing *that* domain of love as well.

And finally, to be realistic we would have to admit that most of our loves have to do with certain fixed relationships that may or may not be within the realm of conscious choice. Frequently the most important loves we have are with those who have a more or less permanent place in our lives—parents, brothers and sisters, husbands and wives, children and other relatives, old friends, sometimes colleagues and neighbors. The problem, in other words, is often not one of *making* relationships, but of understanding the *meaning* of the ones we have. Do I find my self in others with whom I am already situated? It goes without saying that the mere fact that I am connected to others biologically, institutionally, or however, does not necessarily mean that I love them. If Jean-Paul Sartre showed us nothing else, he certainly drove home the point of the individual's power of negation. There are no ties that bind me to another unless I at least tacitly consent to them. Or, to put it more positively, every continuing relationship rests upon some kind of affirmation, implicit or explicit. We can always say no. Sometimes we do—rejection, separation, and abandonment are not uncommon—but more often we do not. The reasons why we continue certain relationships, or decline to reject them, may be impossible to answer. Maybe the reasons are not as important as the actuality—the fact that life itself seems to require us to love. The "isolated I" is hardly anyone's vision of an ideal life.

The question is, how do I sort out the priorities of these relationships? If love is finding myself in another, then hard questions often need to be asked. Do I in fact identify with the other? Does he or she extend or reflect myself in some decisive way? Because she is useful? Because he is open and lets me be myself? Because she is exciting? Because I can depend on him? Because she challenges me? Because he is like a second self? The fact that such expectations are inconsistent with one another does not keep us from wanting them all. Indeed, quite irrationally we often expect *one person* to fulfill them all.

Understanding these different ideas of love might help us to be a little more realistic in what we expect from love by making meanings and implications more clear. But understanding cannot tell us whom to love or how. Here we come up against mystery. Intellectual inquiry ends at this point and affirmation of life begins.

SELECTED BIBLIOGRAPHY

Aiken, Henry David. *Reason and Conduct – New Bearings in Moral Philosophy*. New York: Alfred Knopf, 1962.

Arendt, Hannah. *The Human Condition*. Chicago: University of Chicago Press, 1958.

Augustine. *The Confessions of St. Augustine*. Translated by F. J. Sheed. New York: Sheed & Ward, 1943.

Barth, Karl. *Against the Stream*. London: SCM Press, 1954.

Beauvoir, Simone de. *The Second Sex*. Translated by H. M. Parshley. New York: Bantam Books, 1961.

Bédier, Joseph. *The Romance of Tristan and Iseult*. Translated by Hilaire Belloc, completed by Paul Rosenfeld. New York: Vintage Books, Random House, 1945.

Brooke, C.N.L. *The Medieval Idea of Marriage*. Oxford: Oxford University Press, 1989.

D'Arcy, Martin. *The Mind and Heart of Love*. New York: Henry Holt & Co., 1947.

Dover, K. J. *Greek Homosexuality*. Cambridge, Massachusetts: Harvard University Press, 1978.

Foucault, Michel. *The History of Sexuality*. Vol. 1, *An Introduction*. Translated by Robert Hurley. New York: Vintage Books, Random House, 1980.

——. *The History of Sexuality*. Vol. 2, *The Use of Pleasure*. Translated by Robert Hurley. New York: Vintage Books, Random House, 1986.

Fraser, Nancy and Sandra Lee Bartky, eds. *Revaluing French Feminism*. Bloomington: Indiana University Press, 1992.

Gilson, Étienne. *Heloise and Abelard*. Ann Arbor: University of Michigan Press, 1960.

Gould, Thomas. *Platonic Love*. Glencoe: Free Press, 1963.

Harrison, Verna. *Grace and Human Freedom According to St. Gregory of Nyssa*. Lewiston: Edwin Mellen Press, 1992.

Hatto, A. T. *Gottfried von Strassburg, "Tristan," with the Surviving Fragments of the Tristan of Thomas, Newly Translated. With an Introduction.* Harmondsworth: Penguin, 1960.

Hegel, G.W.F. *The Phenomenology of Mind*. Translated by J. B. Baillie. New York: Harper Torchbook, 1967.

Herman, Barbara. "Could It Be Worth Thinking about Kant on Sex and Marriage?" In *A Mind of One's Own — Feminist Essays on Reason and Objectivity*, edited by Louise M. Antony and Charlotte Witt. Boulder: Westview Press, 1993. 49–67.

Hobbes, Thomas. *Leviathan*. New York: Collier Macmillan, 1962.

Homiak, Marcia L. "Feminism and Aristotle's Rational Ideal." In *A Mind of One's Own — Feminist Essays on Reason and Objectivity*, edited by Louise M. Antony and Charlotte Witt. Boulder: Westview Press, 1993. 1–18.

Irigaray, Luce. *Speculum of the Other Woman*. Translated by Gillian C. Gill. Ithaca: Cornell University Press, 1974.

———. *This Sex Which Is Not One*. Translated by Catherine Porter with Carolyn Burke. Ithaca: Cornell University Press, 1985.

———. *Marine Lover of Friedrich Nietzsche*. Translated by Gillian C. Gill. New York: Columbia University Press, 1991.

———. *An Ethics of Sexual Difference*. Translated by Carolyn Burke and Gillian C. Gill. Ithaca: Cornell University Press, 1993.

Jackson, W.T.H. *The Anatomy of Love*. New York: Columbia University Press, 1971.

Kant, Immanuel. *The Fundamental Principles of the Metaphysics of Morals*. Translated by Thomas K. Abbott, with an introduction by Marvin Fox. New York: Liberal Arts Press, 1949.

———. *Lectures on Ethics*. Translated by Louis Infeld. New York: Harper Torchbooks, 1963.

———. *Doctrine of Virtue*. Part 2 of *The Metaphysics of Morals*. Translated by Mary J. Gregor. Philadelphia: University of Pennsylvania Press, 1964.

Kierkegaard, Søren. *Either/Or — A Fragment of Life*. Abridged and translated by Alastair Hannay. London: Penguin Books, 1992.

———. *Works of Love*. Translated by Howard V. Hong and Edna H. Hong. London: Collins, 1962.

———. *Fear and Trembling and Repetition*. Translated by Howard V. Hong and Edna H. Hong. Princeton: Princeton University Press, 1983.

Kosman, L. A. "Platonic Love." In *Facets of Plato's Philosophy*, edited by W. H. Werkmeister. Assen, Amsterdam: Van Gorcum, 1976.

Lewis, C. S. *The Four Loves*. New York: Harvest Book, Harcourt Brace Jovanovich, 1960.

McKeon, Richard, ed. *Introduction to Aristotle*. 2nd ed., rev. and enl. Chicago: University of Chicago Press, 1973.

Moravcsik, J.M.E. "Reason and Eros in the 'Ascent' Passage of the *Symposium*." In *Essays in Ancient Greek Philosophy*, edited by John P. Anton with George L. Kustas. Albany: SUNY, 1971.

Murdoch, Iris. *Metaphysics as a Guide to Morals*. New York: Allen Lane/ Penguin Press, 1992.

Nygren, Anders. *Agape and Eros*. Translated by Philip S. Watson. Philadelphia: Westminster Press, 1953.

Pagels, Elaine. *Adam, Eve, and the Serpent*. New York: Random House, 1988.

Plato. *Lysis, Socratic Discourses by Plato and Xenophon*. Translated by J. Wright. New York: Everyman's Library, 1910.

——. *Phaedrus*. Translated by W. C. Helmbold and W. G. Rabinowitz. Indianapolis: Library of Liberal Arts, Bobbs-Merrill Co., 1956.

——. *The Republic*. Translated by Desmond Lee, 2nd. ed., rev. Harmondsworth: Penguin Books, 1974.

——. *The Symposium*. Translated by Alexander Nehamas and Paul Woodruff. Indianapolis: Hackett Publishing Co., 1989.

Price, A. W. *Love and Friendship in Plato and Aristotle*. Oxford: Clarendon Press, 1989.

Radice, Betty, trans. *The Letters of Abelard and Heloise*. Harmondsworth: Penguin, 1974.

Rougemont, Denis de. *Love in the Western World*. New York: Pantheon Books, 1956.

Sartre, Jean-Paul. *Existentialism*. Translated by Bernard Frechtman. New York: Philosophical Library, 1947.

——. *No Exit and Three Other Plays*. Translated by Stuart Gilbert. New York: Vintage Books, 1955.

——. *Being and Nothingness*. Translated by Hazel E. Barnes. New York: Washington Square Press, Pocket Books, 1956.

Scruton, Roger. *Sexual Desire – A Moral Philosophy of the Erotic*. New York: Free Press, Macmillan, 1986.

Singer, Irving. *The Nature of Love – Plato to Luther*. New York: Random House, 1966.

——. *The Nature of Love*. Vol. 2, *Courtly and Romantic*. Chicago: University of Chicago Press, 1984.

——. *The Nature of Love*. Vol. 3, *The Modern World*. Chicago: University of Chicago Press, 1987.

Slater, Philip. *The Pursuit of Loneliness*. Boston: Beacon Press, 1970.

Soble, Alan, ed. *Eros, Agape and Philia – Readings in the Philosophy of Love*. New York: Paragon House, 1989.

Thurber, James and E. B. White. *Is Sex Necessary?* New York: Perennial Library, 1957.

Tillich, Paul. *Love, Power, and Justice*. New York: Oxford University Press, 1954.

SOURCES

Quotations that appear in the chapter headings were drawn from the following sources:

"The Mess of Love" by D. H. Lawrence. From *The Complete Poems of D. H. Lawrence*, edited by V. de Sola Pinto & F. W. Roberts. New York: Viking Penguin.

"Lines to a Movement in Mozart's E-Flat Symphony" by Thomas Hardy. From *The Complete Poems of Thomas Hardy*, edited by James Gibson. New York: Macmillan, 1978.

Against the Stream by Karl Barth. London: SCM Press, 1954, page 238.

Tristan by Gottfried of Strasbourg. From *Love in the Western World*, translated by Denis de Rougemont. New York: Pantheon Books, 1956, page 146, note 1.

Sonnet 116 by William Shakespeare.

"September 1, 1939" by W. H. Auden. From *W. H. Auden: Collected Poems*, edited by Edward Mendelson. New York: Random House, 1979.

"Laelius: On Friendship" by Marcus Tullius Cicero. From *Cicero—On the Good Life*, translated by Michael Grant. Harmondsworth: Penguin Books, 1971, page 189.

In Ps. XXXI, En. II by Augustine, Bishop of Hippo. From *An Augustine Synthesis*, arranged by Erich Przywara. New York: Harper Torchbook, 1958, page 341, number 614.

INDEX

About the Author

ROBERT E. WAGONER is Professor of Philosophy at Juniata College.

ISBN 0-275-95839-6

90000>

EAN

9 780275 958398

HARDCOVER BAR CODE